With my best wishes, Kay

HOW I ACHIEVED

My Dream

KARIM W. NASSER

with MAY M. NASSER

(my daughter)

Library and Archives Canada Cataloguing in Publication

Nasser, Karim W. (Karim Wade)
    How I achieved my dream / Karim W. Nasser ; with May M. Nasser.

ISBN 0-88880-498-9

        1. Nasser, Karim W. (Karim Wade). 2. Lebanon--Biography.
I. Nasser, May II. Title.

DS87.2.N38A3 2005   956.9204
C2005-904724-0

Book design by Fred Koop, Saskatoon, SK
Printed in Canada by Apex Graphics Ltd., Saskatoon, SK

Victory Books
350 - 103rd Street East
Saskatoon, SK, S7N 1Z1
CANADA

Dedicated to

My lovely grandchildren Jamie, Aidan, Connor and Rory
The young and young at heart who love to dream
All those who touched our lives

In honour of

My loving aunt Badre

In memory of

My beloved parents, grandparents,
aunt, uncle, and cousin:
Ward, Wadih, Nabiha, Karimeh, Fadlallah,
Jiryes, Marie, Sabih and Elias

Contents

Introduction

T his is the story of a boy growing into manhood and also into
the realization of the fundamental importance of individual
freedom. It is set in the beautiful country of Lebanon before and
during the Depression and World War II and presents a detailed
and fascinating account of life in a time and place which no longer
exists. We first meet Karim at his school recital, singing about the
beauty of a meadowlark's life in the forest, despite its danger, as
opposed to the deadliness of a secure life in a gilded cage. We
follow Karim through his daily life, meet his family and come to
understand the constraints against which he must struggle to find
his own freedom.

Karim leaves his mountain village home to attend school in the
cosmopolitan, vibrant and exotic city of Beirut. The Second World
War, near famine and politics interrupt Karim's academic education
but he continues to learn about life and death, politics, business and
the need to strive against all odds to achieve his goals. Karim
overcomes prejudice and economic distress with the help of his
family and other remarkable and generous people but, ultimately, it
is his own drive and determination that carry him down his chosen
path to achieve his dream and become a visionary professor,
engineer, researcher, inventor, developer, entrepreneur and
philanthropist.

The description of family life in the mountain village of Shweir,
Lebanon is reminiscent of the pioneer life in the early settlement
days of the United States and Canada, but with a Middle Eastern
flavour. The differences in the landscape, vegetation, culture and
lifestyle will be of interest to the reader, young and adult alike.
Likewise, while the main character's development from boy to
man is a universal theme, it is the specifics which set this story
apart and demand attention. The challenges and opportunities
which are presented to the growing youth, and the choices he
makes, are unique to his time and place in modern history.

The characters we meet in this story are fully drawn. Some are
nasty, some are nice, but all are believable, from the Australian

soldier, who saves Karim from drowning, to the American matriarch, who blocks his access to the one thing he most desires.

This is an inspirational and witty story for young people. It shows how they can follow their own vision and dream regardless of the circumstances dealt to them by life, as long as they recognize that they have the freedom to make their own choices. It is the combination of having the liberty to think and act for yourself and also having the drive to press on toward your goal and overcome whatever obstacles are put in your way which can lead each person to their own individual goal, their own idea of success and freedom, their own dream.

M.M. Nasser
Saskatoon, Canada
August 10, 2005

Acknowledgments

We are very grateful to the well known, award winning author and professor, Guy Vanderheaghe, for reviewing the manuscript in spite of his very busy schedule. He made several important suggestions which enhanced this edition.

We are indebted to Telko Sport for allowing us to include some of their photos, to John Waterbury, AUB president, for his AUB Campus photo and to A.G. Kenicer for two photos in Miami, Arizona. We are grateful to the *Saskatoon StarPhoenix* newspaper and the *Green & White* magazine for their permission to reprint some of their articles in this edition. Our thanks are extended to Sharon Hildebrand and her staff for professional printing of the manuscript, to Fred Koop for designing the book, to McNally Robinson Booksellers and Deneen Gudjonson for their help in launching the book.

We are thankful to our dear friend Anwar G. Kenicer, one of the founders of Shweir Foundation and webmaster of Shweir.com, for his persistence in requesting publication of this edition sooner rather than later.

K.W. Nasser & M.M. Nasser

The author's royalties will be donated to the Shweir Scholarship Fund at the American University of Beirut (AUB), the Nasser scholarship funds at the University of Saskatchewan, Kansas University and the American University of Beirut.

Some names have been changed or omitted to protect the privacy of the individuals concerned.

1 Early Childhood in Shweir

T he audience, full of family, friends, and neighbours, was demanding an "encore". The men were stomping their feet and whistling, the women clapping, until the curtain rose and once again silence spread over the room. I, Karim, a chubby, five-year-old boy dressed neatly in a white cotton shirt and red pants, stepped onto the stage. On my shirt, pinned above my heart, was a deep red rose, the petals slightly bruised from the warm hug of my teacher, who had rewarded my performance.

I felt like a giant walking in my own kingdom. My steps on the wooden stage reverberated in my ears like the sound of drums being beaten at a distance. I stopped at center stage and stood with my feet slightly apart. I raised my right hand and recited as loudly as I could the poem I had learned for the school recital, which ended with the following stanza:

I am a free and singing bird
The forest is my home and stage
I would never trade it for a cage
Even if it were made of gold.

Shouts and applause again filled the small room and I bobbed up and down in response and did not notice when my rose dropped to the floor. The friendly crowd began filing out into the street, voices raised as they discussed the school recital. Parents searched for their children, who were emerging from the side entrance. I was one of the first children out the door and dancing straight to my parents who hugged me warmly and kissed me and raved about my performance. It was my mother who noticed the rose was missing and asked me about it. I dashed back to the stage to look for my rose but did not find it. I ran back to my mother and excitedly told her the singing free bird had taken my rose and flown back to the forest, where they both belonged. My parents and the neighbours laughed and began to prepare to go home. I said that I would go home later after I would play a few minutes on the swings with my friends. I barely noticed my mother reminding me to return home before dark, as I was already running full speed towards the playground where my friends were already playing and laughing.

I was named after my widely known and respected paternal grandfather and I lived in a small village, called Shweir, tucked at the foot of Mount Sunnine, Lebanon. The mountain protected the village from the extremes of wind and cold weather. A large forest encircled the village with beautiful pine and oak trees that were in turn well protected by the town's people. Most of the men in the village were craftsmen by tradition, traveling to the neighbouring towns and villages, as well as the larger cities in Lebanon and Syria, to earn their living. The village of Shweir had built a good reputation over the years, especially in masonry construction, and its men were sought after to work on many of the monumental and large structures built in the area and in both countries. The majority of families in the town lived in their own houses, and had small plots of land nearby or on the outskirts of town where they grew their own grains, vegetables and fruits.

When I finally returned home that evening it was later than usual, but I was not disciplined; my normally strict parents were still basking in my performance at the school recital that afternoon. My mother had saved me a bowl of hot soup. After my bath, she tucked me early into bed. My family lived by the principle "early to bed, early to rise". On this particular day, it was especially important that I sleep early as I was to go hunting the next day with my uncle Sabih. The hunting trip was the promised reward for a good performance at the recital. I, however, was unable to sleep, tossing and turning and reliving the day's events. My mind wandered from one thing to another, but always returned to the singing bird that preferred the adventures and risks of the forest to the security of a golden cage. It was a long night for me and when I woke up I could not remember falling asleep — I could only remember feeling the conviction that birds are born to live free in the forest, not imprisoned in a cage. I was equally convinced that my family and my neighbours, my friends and relatives, were also born free like the birds, and if it were not for their love for the same freedom as the birds they would have not responded with such enthusiasm to my poem the day before.

The next morning, when uncle Sabih came by to pick me up for hunting, my mother was unable to wake me up. Sabih did not want to wait and be delayed, as the best time for hunting was early in the morning, so he left instructions for me to meet him later, in the forest near the water spring. It was long past eight in the morning when I finally woke up. I had a quick sandwich of cheese and "zatar" before dashing off towards the forest. Zatar (thyme) is a natural herb that grows in abundance in the forest. It can be eaten fresh or it can be dried, ground and mixed with olive oil, sumach, roasted sesame seeds and salt to form a spread for use in appetizers and for a quick breakfast or snack. It can also be used as a paste in making gourmet pizza because it has a very aromatic, strong, distinctive, tangy and spicy flavour. According to the village legend zatar enhances courage and brightness if it is eaten first thing in the morning. My friends and I loved that pizza especially freshly baked for breakfast.

On my way to the forest, I ran through a valley full of grape vines, fruit and fig trees, and all kinds of plants loaded with flowers and blossoms of all colours which attracted hordes of birds, bees and butterflies, each whispering and singing the story of life which unfolds each spring. A narrow creek wound its way through the valley. Its water was clear and ice cold and the local farmers used its waters to irrigate their orchards, taking turns on a daily rotating basis. Uncle Sabih heard me approaching in the forest and called out to me to follow the creek. I enjoyed hopping from rock to rock, neither tripping nor slipping on the rocks worn smooth over the years by the running water. The creek water percolated joyously downstream, creating a lovely symphony of sounds that lifted the spirits of all who heard it. Uncle Sabih smiled as I successfully worked my way across the creek without slipping.

When I reached the other side of the creek, Uncle Sabih handed me the gun and explained carefully how to aim and pull the trigger. The game that day was birds. I could hear the small creatures chirping and twittering from among the leaves in the trees and I began to tiptoe my way carefully toward the fig trees, listening and concentrating to identify the source of the birds' songs. I silently worked my way to a particularly lush apricot tree and peering closely was able to spy a fat little bird perched on one of the branches. I took aim, adjusted the gun on my shoulder, closed my eyes and pulled the trigger. The blast knocked me back and the smoke and noise filled my head. When I finally opened my eyes, all I could see was some leaves fluttering to the ground and birds darting off in all directions, screaming warnings to any of their nearby friends. Uncle Sabih good-naturedly strolled up and showed me once again how to aim the gun and hold it steady on my shoulder, and most importantly, not to close my eyes before pulling the trigger. On my ninth try, I finally felled a stray bird. I was terribly proud of my achievement but, as I strolled home with my uncle, I could not help reflecting whether it would not have been better for the bird to be caged and safe rather than free and shot dead like that. I asked my uncle what he thought about birds and whether they were better off free or caged. Sabih hesitated, and then told me that wild birds tasted better than caged birds. Why should they, I asked. The wild birds were skinnier and my mother often said that hens from the coop tasted better than any skinny birds from the forest.

I spent my summer of long beautiful idle days running with my friends and thinking of nothing more than beating my friends to the best tree in the playground, playing at being birds, eating fruit, singing and surveying all we could see from our preferred vantage point. But the summer days passed quickly and soon it was time for school to start again.

I enjoyed school. There were fascinating stories, arithmetic riddles, bums to pinch, paper birds to fly, chalk for throwing and countless games to play behind the teacher's back. There was also the occasional strapping for those who were caught misbehaving. The school had only one room for all the students; the same teacher taught all levels and the younger children were able to listen to the lessons for the older students. The teacher had to be both diplomatic and firm in order to maintain strict discipline and keep a learning atmosphere present in the schoolroom. Naturally, there were occasions when discipline failed and the room was overcome with laughter. A good source of the mirth came at the attempts by late children to come up with excuses for their tardiness. "My mother said I am not learning anything at school and I should help instead to milk the cows". "My father needed help to fix the fence so our bull would not run away". "I had to go and borrow eggs from our neighbours for breakfast", "I had to help my sister fetch water from the well to water the cows", etc.

It normally took three years to graduate from the school, that is, as soon as one had mastered the ability to read and write and do arithmetic, as set out in the books, which were handed down from one generation of students to the next. It was gradually becoming easier for each generation to pass the arithmetic section, as each succeeding year there were fewer pages to contend with. The principal was careful to give the thinner books to the non-gifted students, thereby giving them the chance to graduate with the more talented students.

In fact, the teacher had to have many talents, as well as diplomacy, to cope with the day-to-day demands of the one room school. The school had to be kept clean, books glued back together, disputes settled, wounds bandaged, etc. Outside of the classroom, the teacher had to be creative with eggs and potatoes as payment of his salary was made up mostly of these food items. The teacher was proud of his cooking ability and boasted that he had more recipes for eggs than any chicken ever dreamt off. He was particularly fond of swallowing them whole and raw from the shell so that he did not have to cook, smell or taste them.

Then in 1938, the school year was cut short. The teacher had received from his uncle a letter and immigration papers from the United States of America. He had been accepted to immigrate to the USA and was going to move to Miami, Arizona to help run his uncle Saad Rayes' grocery store. When the pupils and their parents learned of their teacher's upcoming move, they began to bring the teacher gifts. The one he seemed to value most was a miniature eagle in flight carved from local stone by my grandfather Fadlallah who was also residing in Miami since the 1910s. Before he left for America, the teacher gave the eagle to me for safekeeping as he could carry only a minimum of baggage with him to the new country. When giving me the eagle, he advised me to be sure to complete my education at the university in Beirut, as education would make me as free as the eagle itself.

Once I was out of school, after the teacher's departure, I helped my mother in our garden at the edge of town. I daydreamed while weeding, about the birds, bees, butterflies and lizards in the forest. I enjoyed nursing the garden and watching it develop, from tiny seeds, to blossoms, to tomatoes, beans, sweet peas, cucumbers, squash, potatoes, etc. which in turn produced the seeds for the next season. I also watched the birds build their nests from dry grass and small branches and lay their eggs and hatch them. I was thrilled when the baby birds were born and kept a close eye on them as their parents fed them until they learned to fly. In contrast, I would think of our own chicken and their coop and the chicken eggs that had been given to my teacher, who had been too poor to refuse them and needed the eggs to keep from going hungry.

With the teacher gone, most of the students began to go to work with their fathers to learn a trade. My father, Wadih, or Abu Karim, the traditional nickname given to the father of a son named Karim, mentioned in passing one day that he thought I ought to continue with school, as an education would be better than learning a trade. That was not the usual routine in the village. I was the oldest of seven children and according to tradition I should be prepared to work with my father so that the two of us could earn enough to support the whole family.

One evening, after having pondered my father's comment for a few days, I told my parents I would like to continue with my studies as long as the family did not need me to help provide for them. On hearing my statement, my father straightened himself up on his chair and cleared his throat. My brother and sisters focused attentively on their father. This would be an important announcement. My father started by stating that education is a valuable asset in the hands of the right person, but it could become a burden if one became intoxicated and arrogant from the education and lost sight of its significance. He continued on to say that he had seen many educated arrogant guys in the village but he had full confidence in me and he was sure that I would do well. Nevertheless, education was a very expensive proposition and the whole family would have to tighten its belt for several years to support me at school. After a long silence my mother then suggested we could ask her brother Sabih to help by providing lodging in the city, where he worked and lived with his mother and sisters, Marie and Badre. She volunteered to write to Sabih if my father approved of the idea. After some hesitation, my father agreed to the proposal, although he knew Sabih and his mother Imm Sabih, Nabiha, and sisters lived in a one-room apartment. I was elated and bubbly at hearing my father's approval and jumped up and hugged and kissed each of my parents very warmly, thanking them for their encouragement and help. That evening I did not go to bed until I had begged and worried and made sure my mother had written a letter to her brother as she volunteered to do so.

Early the next morning, I carried the letter to the village post office located in the Basha residence on the northwest corner of the village square. I banged on the door a few times and listened carefully, hoping to hear the deep voice and heavy footsteps of Mr. Basha from behind the heavy, solid wooden door. But there was only silence. I banged again with all my strength, not noticing the pain in my knuckles. After a few short moments, which seemed very long moments indeed to me, a black cat appeared at one of the windows and settled on the windowsill, lazily wagging its tail and meowing while eyeing me with fierce eyes. I felt this was really a bad omen, as my grandmother had told me that black cats were the messengers of the forest witches. I felt deflated even though I had always questioned the superstitious beliefs of the village people. I was about to give up and leave, when Mrs. Basha suddenly appeared in the window, picked up the black cat and stroked her lightly from the tips of her ears to the tip of the tail. When Mrs. Basha saw me, she put down her cat and came to open the door.

"What are you up to, so early in the morning?" she asked. I showed her my letter and excitedly told her it was urgent that the letter be mailed immediately to my uncle and I begged Mrs. Basha to make sure my uncle responded to the letter the same day. At this, Mrs. Basha reflected a few seconds, as if trying to imagine uncle Sabih's response to the urgent request for an immediate answer. She looked sullenly at me and began to explain that her husband had gone to the locksmith to fetch a new key for the stamp drawer. She could not help me until Mr. Basha returned with the key to unlock the drawer. She and her husband had been visiting Mr. Basha's sister and her family of nine children and Mrs. Basha was convinced that one of her nieces or nephews had lost the key while playing with Mr. Basha's key ring. Mrs. Basha then sent me home, telling me I could come back in the afternoon or, better yet, tomorrow. I was terribly disappointed and I knew the disappointment showed on my face, but Mrs. Basha simply closed the door, the sullen look still on her face.

I turned away with a heavy heart and wondered what to do next. As I walked away, dragging my feet, I looked at the letter in my hand and wished there were an alternative to the government mail service and especially to its agent, Mrs. Basha, who was thought to be too crazy and unfriendly to be entrusted with the villagers' mail. Many of my neighbours had curtailed their letter writing to avoid having to go to the post office and face the piercing looks of Mrs. Basha and fend off her unfriendly questions.

As I was unhappily crossing the street to return home, I spotted Nassib, my father's first cousin, standing at the bus stop. Nassib was dressed in his Sunday suit and carrying a large, well-filled white bag by its tassels. He greeted me warmly and asked me why was I up and about so early in the morning. I returned the greeting and explained that I was trying to send a letter to my uncle Sabih in Beirut, but Mrs. Basha had refused to mail it for me. Nassib smiled and told me that he was on his way to the tobacco factory where Sabih worked. He then offered to deliver the letter by hand for me. My face brightened and I handed the letter over for delivery. I then eagerly asked Nassib to please, please ask Sabih to respond right away. Nassib agreed, tucked the letter in his front pocket and told me not to worry — the letter would be safely delivered into Sabih's hands. The bus appeared and as Nassib boarded, I shouted my thanks; he looked back to see me waving happily after him. Nassib found his seat and as the bus pulled away he waved at me until the bus and Nassib disappeared down the road, which wound its way out of town through the grove of tall trees.

I spent the rest of the day playing with my friends, but I felt it was the longest day of my life. I kept checking the location of the sun in the sky, but it would not set despite my longing that it would do so. I had told my friends about the letter and some of them could not resist using the opportunity to tease me. Elias, one of my friends, told me he had heard the bus driver's wife tell her neighbour that her husband would not be returning to their village that evening as he had to repair the brakes of the bus. I did not believe my friend and managed to keep calm even as the sun began to set and there was yet no sign of the dust on the horizon, nor had I heard the sound of the horn that usually announced the approach of the bus. It was the bus driver's habit to honk his horn several times the minute he arrived at the edge of the village to allow those who wanted to meet the bus to make their way to the central stop. Some villagers would come to meet their relatives and carry their baggage, others to pick up parcels they were expecting from friends and relatives. The bus was their main link between the village and Beirut, due to the villagers' avoidance of Mrs. Basha and the post office.

That evening, the bus was delayed and arrived in the village later than usual. I was on my way to the bus driver's house to inquire after the bus when I heard the horn blowing at the edge of town. I sped to Nassib's house, which was near the central stop, and waited, my heart beating furiously. When Nassib appeared at the door of the bus, I ran over to greet him warmly, my eyes shining hopefully. Nassib looked kindly down at me and explained that he had indeed delivered the letter to Sabih. Yet, he could not wait for Sabih's answer, as there was family shopping to do before the bus returned to town. My heart sank and my face darkened. But I thanked Nassib anyway and trudged home quietly.

I found my five sisters and Fadlallah, my younger brother, at home alone. My father was still at work and my mother was working in the family garden plot at the edge of town. I sat dejectedly on the front steps of our house and rested my chin on my hands, which in turn rested on my knees. I was sad and would not respond to my sisters' giggling and teasing. It was Noha, my youngest sister, who pushed herself up against my knees until I hugged her and began to talk again. Najla, Juliet, Karimeh, Soumaya and Fadlallah continued to banter and play on the steps in front of both of us.

This is how my parents found their seven children when they both returned home shortly after sunset. I was still hugging Noha, trying to keep her from crying. By now, Noha was upset because of the late return of our parents. When I saw my parents, I told them how my letter had been delivered but the answer would be delayed. My father hugged me warmly and assured me it would not be long before Sabih responded. My mother also hugged me warmly and agreed, saying it takes time to write a letter and Sabih was always busy at work during the day. She then clapped her hands and ordered us to wash our hands and get ready for dinner. I mumbled softly to myself, but as there was nothing I could do about the letter, I did as I was told and got ready for dinner.

That evening, we sat down to a deep bowl of kidney beans cooked in a thick sauce of lemon, olive oil, garlic and spices, with fresh parsley sprinkled liberally over the top. Najla brought a pile of thin, flattened loaves of bread to the table and distributed them around the bowl of "bezr loubieh". My mother brought in a handful of raw, peeled red onions and placed them on the table with the bread. There were neither spoons nor forks on the table; we ate dinner by tearing small pieces of bread from the loaves and folding them to scoop the beans and sauce by the mouthful. Each one of us would then pop a small piece of the raw onion into our mouth for every mouthful of beans. This food is one of the most delicious dinners as well as one of the staple meals in the village. My parents helped the three younger children, who had not yet mastered the art of using the bread as a spoon but the rest of us had to fend for ourselves. It wasn't rare to find several pairs of hands in a tangle above the full bowl, and the beans and sauce often failed to make it from the bowl to waiting mouth, much to the chagrin of my mother, known in the village as Imm Karim (the mother of Karim), though her real name was Ward. The light plop of food landing on the table was sometimes followed by a light slap on a wrist as my mother tried to make us children behave and be quiet for the course of the meal.

I did not eat well that night, even though bezr loubieh was one of my favourite dishes. My parents seemed to understand my lack of appetite and did not insist as they usually would that I eat well and finish my meal. When it was time for bed, my mother spread the cotton mattresses on the floor and I slipped into bed right away. I pulled the blanket over my head and turned my back on my younger brother, who shared the bed with me. That evening Fadlallah seemed to sense that it would be better not to tease me as he usually would and instead poked and tickled Noha, who slept in the next bed with Karimeh.

The next day, our routine began early, as usual. My parents awoke early, as soon as our proud, red rooster ushered in the day with its beautiful song. My mother went directly to the back room to fetch the bran, which she mixed with water and put out in the yard for the chickens.

She next gathered the eggs from the chicken coop and prepared breakfast for my father and packed his lunch. Immediately after breakfast, my father left for work, as a stone mason. My mother awakened the older children next and she sent two of us to fill the water jugs at one of the village wells. The rest of the family would wash first and then have breakfast. Once we completed these daily activities, my mother ordered us to go either to school or to play with our friends in the neighbouring fields. I did not have school that day so I told my mother I would go to the creek to play with my friends. I stopped at Elias' house, next door, and the two of us began the trek to the creek together. On the way, we stopped to pick up Wadih and we three then began to run to the creek. The road weaved between the village houses and skirted an abandoned and partly ruined house at the edge of town. The doors and windows of this house had long since been removed and the roof had caved in. As we approached the ruined house, Wadih suggested we go in and see if the eggs in the meadowlarks' nest inside had hatched yet. We were cautiously entering the building when a cat jumped away from the nest, where it had been eyeing the eggs; we were startled immediately. However, Elias calmed us down, picked a few stones and pitched them after the cat and chased it for a few yards, but the cat disappeared before his stones could find their mark.

We turned back to the nest, which was tucked in a corner near the ceiling. The cat had been perched on one of the windowsill and would have had to jump quite a distance to reach the nest. It seemed to us that the eggs would be safe from the cat — all we could see from where we stood was the head of one of the meadowlarks, turning this way and that, surveying the usually empty house. Wadih wanted to throw stones at the nest to frighten the meadowlark, but I talked him out of that idea, as there was the chance the stones might crack the eggs or hit one of the baby birds if they had hatched. There being nothing else to do in the house, we continued on our way to the creek. When we arrived at the cliff overlooking the creek we lined up to slide down the steep slope one at a time. Each one let out his own personalized "battle cry" as he slid down, competing to be loudest. The creek at the bottom was neither large nor very deep and we could cross from one bank to the other easily, using smooth rocks as stepping-stones. There were also two ponds, trees, grass and shrubs in the area that afforded plenty of fun not least of which were the frogs, which nested in the pond to the side of one of the bushes.

We thought that the dominant male frog actually seemed friendly and we had nicknamed him "Bunso" due to his particularly large belly. Bunso would squat at the bottom of the pond and survey the outside world with inquisitive, fearless eyes. The rest of the frog troop would quickly disappear into the thick layer of mud at the bottom of the pond when we appeared at the edge of the pond. That morning, we gathered around the pond, hoping to see Bunso. We had unearthed a long, juicy worm and impaled it on the end of a thin twig to tempt Bunso. Although the worm was twitching prettily near the bottom of the pond, and Elias called out for Bunso to come up, Bunso remained out of sight. Finally, Elias dropped the stick with the worm into the pond and we three tried to dash back up the steep hill, challenging each other to make the climb without falling back to the bottom and without using our hands to crawl up. I was the first to succeed, after each boy had failed a number of times and Wadih and Elias managed the feat shortly thereafter. When we three arrived at the top of the hill, we were joined by several more friends from the village and the whole joyful gang began the endless fun of sliding down and crawling back up the hill until we were exhausted. Then, all of us trooped around the creek bank until we came to a sheltered area of a large bush of sweet potatoes. After pulling up a few plants and cutting off the plump, whitish bulbs, we heaped the potatoes in a pile at the edge of the creek and sat down, dangling our feet in the cool water, to enjoy a small feast. There we sat until Najm's mother could be heard calling him to get home and deliver his father's lunch to him at work. Najm's departure was the beginning of the end and the whole gang of friends soon after began to make our separate ways home for lunch.

After lunch, our group of friends met again at the schoolyard where we began a game of soccer. The ball was made out of old rags sewn together in the appropriate shape. I played well as it was a sport I loved. My favourite position was center offence. This particular afternoon I scored two goals, which helped my team beat the other team by a score of 5 to 4. My team mates crowded around me after my second goal, cheering, shouting, and congratulating me on gaining the ball and scoring after a hard fought battle near the goal of the opposing team. Chafic and Bahij of the opposing team complained that the goal was foul and left the game when no one listened to their complaint.

The next morning, I accompanied my mother to the family garden plot at the edge of the village. We encountered several of the neighbours on the way, but it was my mother's conversation with one in particular, Mrs. Salimeh that caught my attention. Mrs. Salimeh was giving her forecast for this year's crops and stated with authority that as the seven leaves she used in her forecasting had become bone dry in an unusually short time, it was going to be a poor year for crops. Once Mrs. Salimeh was out of earshot, I demanded of my mother whether she believed Mrs. Salimeh. My mother looked surprised and said of course she did. She defended Mrs. Salimeh, saying that her forecasting abilities were particularly good even though she had never attended university; her forecasts, asserted my mother, were as good as or even better than those of

Professor Jurdak, the expert meteorologist at the American University of Beirut, one of the very few educated people from our village. With that said, my mother and I continued on our way, chatting about other matters.

When we arrived at the garden plot, I went on to the water reservoir to draw water. The reservoir was built on a high spot at the far end of the garden. Gravity helped the water flow from a hole in the bottom of the reservoir into a ditch which in turn led into a series of furrows that led to the rows of vegetables in the garden. I could release the water by grabbing hold of a stick, which protruded vertically from the surface of the water, and manoeuvring it around to break the mud seal, which held the water in. The water soon began to gush from the opening at the bottom of the reservoir into the ditch.

My job that day was to water the cherry, apple, pear and plum trees in the eastern area of the garden. My mother planted beans, peas, parsley, radishes, lettuce, tomatoes, cucumber, eggplant, potatoes, garlic, onions and squash, to name a few. When she was ready to plant the tomatoes and cucumbers, she called me over to help. She had earlier promised me I would be able to plant my own plants and care for them during the growing season. I watched while my mother dug a small ditch with her hand spade, dropped a few seeds into the ditch every two feet and then covered them with about one inch of soil. For the tomato plants, she dug a hole with the spade, placed the roots of the plant deep into the hole, again covered the roots with soil and pressed the soil down with her hand. She would later lay three large mulberry leaves over the plants to protect them from the harsh rays of the sun until she was sure the plants would be able to grow on their own.

I was excited at the prospect of planting my own cucumbers and tomatoes. Once I had completed my rows, my mother and I irrigated the rest of the garden, and then spread chicken manure, which we had brought from our chicken coop, in the furrows where we had placed seeds or plants. Because the manure would draw in moisture from the soil, it would not blow away with the wind.

When the water reservoir was empty, I went to close up the opening, without telling my mother what I was doing. I grabbed some handfuls of clay from beside the reservoir and, by mixing the clay with water, made a large plastic mass of clay to plug the hole. I climbed into the reservoir and forced the wet clay into the hole around the wooden stick. It would soon swell and recreate the seal to hold the water in the reservoir. I then tried to climb out of the reservoir by hooking my fingers over the edge of the reservoir wall and using my feet to propel myself towards the top. I was half way up the wall when my fingers slipped and I fell flat on my back in the mud and shallow water at the bottom of the reservoir. Furious and anxious to clean myself of the mud, I hopped around the reservoir until I noticed my mother peering into my eyes with a look of surprise on her face.

"What happened?" she asked.

I started to explain, crying and laughing a little at the same time and my mother soon joined in. The giggles and tears soon stopped and my mother reached in to help me crawl out of the reservoir. With my mother's help I cleaned myself as well as I could and we turned to walk back through the garden, occasionally breaking into laughter. As I had no clean clothes to change into, my mother finally suggested that I take my clothes off and let them hang in a plum tree to dry in the sun. I could then sit in the shade of the nearby bushes while my mother finished her work in the garden. About an hour later, the clothes dried and the garden work finished, my mother and I headed back home. I was careful to avoid talking to any of my neighbours, as I did not want anyone to notice how dirty I was.

Working in the garden was part of the daily routine from April through September. The only exception was Sundays, as every one in the family had to go to church. The garden work changed gradually as the plants grew and passed from one growth stage into another. After the harvest, we had to keep working in the garden until the fall in order to have the land cleaned, tilled and ready for next spring. However, we kids, always found time to fool around, play soccer and other games whenever we could get away without doing any chores.

First Trip to Beirut to Attend Elementary School

A few days later, I was playing soccer with my friends against a team of boys from the southern end of the village. Some of the boys from the "southern" team were older and during the game tried to throw their weight around, resulting in a heated match as we the younger boys fought hard to hold our own. To the great joy of my team, the final score was tied at 2-2. We hid our feelings until the other team had wandered away so as not to excite them. As soon as the last of the southerners had disappeared down the alley, my friends and I let our hilarity break out and we began to make our own delirious way home.

As we were walking, I heard my second cousin Edmond shout, "Hey, there is your uncle Sabih".

I immediately took off in the direction Edmond was pointing, and Edmond and several other boys followed me to my uncle; I had not expected to see Sabih for several more days. On hearing my voice, Sabih turned around.

He hugged and kissed me warmly and said, "I have returned early with your grandmother "Sitto" and aunts because your grandfather "Jiddo" has taken seriously ill. I'm on my way to fetch Dr. "Milhem".

I was left standing still in shock as I watched Sabih hurry towards the home of the only doctor in the village. My heart was pounding with anxiety and I put my hand over my heart to keep it from dropping into my stomach. As Sabih rounded the corner and disappeared from sight, I turned and sped for home, leaving my friends to themselves. When I entered home, my mother grabbed me and instructed me in a whisper to be very quiet and go to bed right away. She did not want me or my brother and sisters to disturb our Jiddo, who seemed to be resting at that moment. I asked for and got permission to peak in on my Jiddo before going to bed. I could already hear my Jiddo's heavy breathing from the other room.

My Grandfather was sleeping in the metal bed and his eyes were closed. My father was sitting in a wooden chair next to the bed. On a nearby table there were a bottle of medicine, a jug of lemonade and a glass, which was half full. My Sitto came in at that moment. She took my hand and led me over to the side of the bed to look at my resting grandfather. Then, she told Jiddo that I was there and wanted to say Hi; Jiddo opened his eyes slightly and smiled. I tried to talk to Jiddo but I could not find any words to say to him but mumbled something incomprehensible mixed with my tears and sniffles while hanging and pressing into Jiddo's hand. Jiddo pulled me closer to him and turned sideways in his bed to face me. His face looked puffed, reddish and shiny. I kissed his hand and smothered it with my warm tears and tried to hang onto it as long as I could. Finally, my Sitto interceded, patted me on the head and grabbed my hand and together with Sitto, we walked back to the other room where my grandmother kissed me warmly and asked me to go to bed right away. Sensing the gravity of the situation, I did as I was told. Once in bed, I pulled the covers over my head and prayed to God, Jesus and Mary to make my Jiddo better and let him recover soon.

Neither my prayers, nor the family's prayers, nor the ministrations of Dr. Milhem were good enough. The next morning, my brother and my sisters and I were awakened real early and were instructed to put on our Sunday best clothes and go next door to Haifa's, Elias' mother, for breakfast. Our grandfather had passed away during the night and now our mother and grandmother were going to be too busy to get the breakfast ready and look after us. The death of our grandfather came as a shock to all the family especially the children. We had not seriously understood the severity of our grandfather's illness. Najla and I and the older children were subdued and sad but the younger ones had less comprehension and were happy with the arrangement that would let them play with their friends early in the morning.

Imm Dawood, Imm Nassib and a few other women relatives had washed Grandpa's body, groomed him and dressed him in a neat, pressed black Sherwal suit and white shirt. The men in the house moved the metal bed to the center of the room where the women then covered it with a white sheet before the men placed the body on the bed. Above his head, on the metal bed's grill, they tied a wooden cross, on which a white ribbon was strung. His feet were tied together with a white ribbon and flowers were placed around his body.

Soon, I could see my aunts and my uncle, dressed fully in black, making their way to my parents' house. They looked grim and sad as they hurried towards the deathbed, as though the sky was falling down on Jiddo's body and they needed to prop it up to prevent it from hurting him. I went to watch their activities through a side window. I could see my relatives bringing chairs from the neighbours' homes and arranging them in the two rooms. On several occasions during the day, the chairs would be arranged and rearranged as people tried to keep busy.

Every now and then, a few of the neighbours would stop and talk among themselves. Orders were issued, furniture moved, orders re-issued and furniture moved again, as more people came in, milled about and got involved. The chairs were rearranged, once again, around the bed but far enough back that mourners could pass by the bedside and view the body.

As more neighbours arrived, they brought in more chairs with coloured ribbons tied on the chair legs to help in later identification. The death had been announced in the village that morning by the ringing of the church bells; intermittent peals distinguished the death knoll from the call to mass. Messengers had gone out to the neighbouring villages to inform the mayors of Grandpa's death. All work in the village was cancelled for that day. Only the food stores were open but they closed at noon. The closures were the traditional response to death and few exceptions were tolerated. Relatives, neighbours and friends took on the chores of my family and looked after our needs. They prepared meals, brought them in on trays and left them in the main room for the mourners to eat throughout the long day.

The front rows of chairs were reserved for my family, particularly the women. Throughout the day, they would chant religious songs, weep and recall the events of Jiddo's life. They would ask Jiddo to take with him their love and messages of best regards to loved ones who had passed on before him. The sound of tears and mourning would ebb and rise again as people arrived and passed on their condolences. For some women, the tears could be called up at will. For others, their strength was in chanting the praises of the deceased. Others would murmur quietly in the background, supporting the main mourners and the rest would gather in the corners, gossiping about everybody and laughing nonchalantly.

The men were gathering at the next-door homes of Khalil Abu Kheir and Abu Dawood, where my family sat together in inner corners of the reception rooms, standing up to greet mourners and speaking in sad and subdued tones. There was a steady flow of people and as the rooms filled, the early arrivals would move out to the yard, making room for others in the house. Generally, the men praised Jiddo for his abilities, his strength and his good role as a father, even though he had lately enjoyed drinking. My father and my uncle shed some tears but their mourning could not compare to the outpouring of emotions and tears taking place among the women. Nor were the men's conversation limited to mourning only. They discussed municipal problems, street cleaning, preparing the cemetery for the funeral procession, seeding their crops, even the tomato plants Michel Shaya had brought from Beirut. Michel had bragged that his new plants, a new breed from the University nursery, would mature two weeks earlier than the regular tomato plants. Two teenage boys, one carrying a tray of cigarettes and the other carrying jugs of water, wandered around offering cigarettes and water to those who wanted to drink and smoke. Later, the water would be replaced with coffee.

Shortly before 11:00, the sound of mournful chanting was carried into the Abu Kheir house from the northwest direction. The men looked at each other questioningly, wondering about the source of the sound. Emil, one of my many cousins, came running to announce that a delegation from the neighbouring village of Ain El Sindianeh had arrived and was working its way through the town towards our house. The men quickly moved outside, assembling themselves behind the elders, and went to meet the incoming mourners. The two parties of mourners met at Ain Al-Tahtah water well in the main street in front of the Kiameh store and residence, two blocks down from our residence. Greetings were exchanged and the bereaved family and friends then walked together to the house. The group chanted prayers as they walked and then entered the main room and gathered around Jiddo's body. Gradually, the chanting subsided, only to be replaced by the wailing of the mourning women. The men left the room in twos and threes, as though being pushed out by the women's voices, and immediately gravitated back to the Abu Kheir's house, where the atmosphere of cigarettes and coffee better suited their mourning style.

At noon, lunch was served to all who were present. The food had been prepared by different neighbours and brought steaming hot to the rooms where the mourners were gathered, with the exception of the death room. Service followed, with the elders eating first, and the children last. Later in the afternoon, at 2:30, the priest and his assistant arrived. Father Hanna offered his condolences to all the relatives, received a plate of food and sat beside Sabih, who was Grandpa's only son. They talked quietly for half an hour until the priest stood and whispered to the elders closest to him to follow his lead. This was the signal for the family that it was time to start with the funeral service. Father Hanna led the way into the room where Jiddo lay and all who had gathered stood and followed the priest. The women who had kept the tearful vigil over Grandpa moved to one side to make room for the priest and the other mourners.

Father Hanna stood next to Jiddo's bed and began his prayers. His assistant, Brother Philip, who had a beautiful voice, stood next to him and together the two religious men filled the room with solemn prayers. There was no sound except their voices, and through the quiet, the mourners could hear the roosters crowing and dogs barking in the distance and birds twittering in the trees outside the house. The bedside prayer was brief. Once it was over, several of the neighbours carried in the casket and set it down beside the bed. They then lifted Grandpa's body and gently laid him in the casket. The priest then turned and walked out of the mourning room, lined up his altar boys and made sure one was carrying the cross and the other two held the candles. The funeral procession was about to begin.

The casket was carried by six of the young village men, who were accompanied by the sounds of weeping and prayers. As several of the older village women emerged from the house they shouted out personal messages to Grandpa. The neighbourhood children had lined the street to watch the funeral procession. I stood among them, watching attentively. At times, I would point to special details and whisper to my friends to pay attention. The procession was led by one of the town's policemen, who was followed by the altar boys with the cross and the candles, teenage boys carrying wreaths and bouquets of flowers, twelve teenage girls carrying their prayer books and walking with their teacher, who kept a close eye on them, a group of village women, with four of them carrying together a velvet cloth bearing the image of the Virgin Mary with the Christ child on her lap, the village music band of young men, with one of them holding a flag decorated with the image of a lion, Father Hanna and brother Philip, the six men bearing the casket, surrounded by the relief, the men of the Nasser family, the male neighbours and villagers who had neither a direct tie to the Nasser family nor a specific duty in the funeral and finally, the women of the Nasser family and the other village women.

As the procession wound its way through the village, the young men sang mourning songs, played their musical instruments and chanted prayers. As the procession passed the Abu Akl residence, Nazira Abu Akl leaned out of her second floor window to wave good-bye to Jiddo and to ask him to take care of her young brother who had died two years ago of bronchitis. As the procession approached the one or two village shops that had remained open that day, the owners hurried out, locked their stores behind them and joined the procession. The church bells tolled until the procession reached the front doors of the church. The children, including myself, had been following the funeral procession, sometimes dashing ahead via our favourite shortcuts to get ahead of the mourners and climb to a nearby roof for a better view.

As the church was too small to hold all the mourners, only family members and close friends were able to enter for the service. The rest of the villagers gathered outside, to listen through the open doors and windows. The casket had been placed in front of the altar where the men had congregated. The church was elevated in the rear to a level about three feet from the ground, and this was where the women gathered, in an area reserved for them. Father Hanna conducted an all male choir and with the assistance of his altar boys and the choir led the mourners through the half-hour funeral ceremony. Toward the end of the ceremony, two elderly women walked up to the casket to open it and unbutton the jacket and shirt in which Jiddo had been dressed. Once they had exposed his chest, Father Hanna anointed Grandpa's body with holy oil, making a mark in the shape of the cross. The villagers believed that if the sign of the cross was not made directly on the exposed chest, many more deaths would soon follow in the same family and town. Once the priest had anointed Jiddo, the casket was closed again. Father Hanna then turned and walked out the church doors into the courtyard where the rest of the mourners were gathered. The pallbearers lifted the casket and followed Father Hanna through the courtyard and on toward the cemetery which was two miles east of the church. Many of the elderly mourners stayed behind, knowing that the two-mile walk would be too much for them. It was sunset when the funeral cortege reached the cemetery. The casket was lowered to the ground beside the mausoleum. Jiddo's close friends took turns eulogizing and speaking about his achievements and contributions to his family and the village and offering their condolences to the family. Father Hanna then intoned the last prayers, ending with the words "earth to earth and ashes to ashes". When the prayers were finished, the casket was placed in the grave, a small windowless room with a square wooden door just big enough to allow the casket to be pushed through. Each mausoleum could hold six caskets. On the side of the mausoleum was a pit with a chimney where old remains could be burned and reduced to ashes. The nine largest families in the village each had their own mausoleum, nine identical structures differing only by the engraving on the front. The deceased from the smaller village families would be interred in whichever mausoleum had room at the time.

Many of the children, including myself, were already in the cemetery when the funeral procession arrived after the church service and we watched the final ceremony with interest. As my uncle Sabih and my father stood by the side to receive the final expression of sympathy from the gathered mourners, I squeezed myself in between them to be close to my uncle to console him and to be able to hear the murmured words and shake the occasional hand. Finally, after the last handshake and the last story about the goodness of my Grandpa, my uncle Sabih and the rest of the family turned away from the mausoleum where Jiddo lay and began to walk silently home. I held uncle Sabih's hand firmly, knowing that my uncle understood how sad I felt without yet having said a single word. When the mourners returned home, they found the scent of coffee had filled the house. The family found chairs to sit in while they received condolences from friends and neighbours. Coffee and sweets were served and the early evening passed quietly, with people discussing among themselves the beauty and simplicity of the funeral service, who had shown up from the nearby villages, Father Hanna's eulogy, the hair and clothes of the women and anything else that had caught their attention during the long day of mourning.

Dinner was served at 7:00 PM, and the quiet conversations continued through the meal. Once everyone had eaten, it was time to return the chairs and tables to the neighbouring houses they had come from. Those who had eaten stayed to help clean up and get the house back in order. My sisters and brother and I did our share, delivering the smaller items we could handle by ourselves. We were soon sent away, however, to the next door Abu Kheir home, where we had been invited to spend the night, leaving enough beds in our house for my parents, my Grandma, uncle and aunts. Only Grandpa's bed would remain vacant that night and it would remain unused for the following 40 days to ensure that Jiddo would not feel quickly forgotten after his death. According to the village tradition, anyone who slept in Jiddo's bed before the 40 days had elapsed could expect to suffer horrible nightmares, courtesy of Grandpa's ghost.

Not all the cleaning was completed that night. The next morning, my extended family, the Abu Kheirs, the Shayas, the Eids, the Naders, the Toumas, the Khenaissers and the Sawayas returned to clean up any leftovers. My sisters and brother and I stayed away from home most of the day, appearing only occasionally to retrieve a toy, have a drink or complain about each other. I did not wander too far, however, preferring to remain within earshot with my friends, Elias and Wadih. Uncle Sabih came by in the afternoon and watched us boys at play until he was called home to receive expressions of sympathy from Mikhail, a teacher at a religious school in Sabih's neighbourhood in Beirut. A few minutes later, Uncle Sabih stood at the door and called me to come in and meet Mikhail.

I ran and entered the room in which the men were sitting just as Mikhail was finishing his coffee. After introducing myself and shaking hands with Mikhail, I sat down and looked quizzically at the two men. Mikhail smiled at me and told me that Uncle Sabih had asked him if his school would be able to accept me as a student. Mikhail said he would need to see my school marks before giving his opinion. Excitedly, I said that I did well in school and ran to find my mother to ask for my school report. My mother could not find the report and asked me to help her look. I in turn could not find it either and soon Uncle Sabih had joined in the search, again without any success. Eventually, even Mikhail got involved in looking for my report and it was Mikhail who finally located the report, near the top of the first pile of papers we had all looked in. Mikhail returned to his seat with the report and began to read through it. I followed closely behind, my heart beating faster than usual.

After a few minutes, Mikhail looked up at me and smiled. He patted my shoulder and told me my grades were good and I would likely have no difficulty getting into the school in Beirut where Mikhail taught. I jumped up in joy and ran to Uncle Sabih's side, begging him to let me live with him and go to school in the city. I promised to be a good boy and to listen well to him and abide by all the rules of the household. Uncle Sabih agreed to let me stay with his family on a trial basis for one trimester. I jumped for joy and kissed my uncle warmly, thanking him for his approval and thanking Mikhail for his encouragement. I then ran out of the house, jumping and shouting to my friends that I would be going to school in Beirut.

The boys were all excited to hear the news and began to imagine what the school would look like and how exciting and different it would be to live in the city instead in their small village. We discussed the tall buildings, how many more cars, bicycles, donkeys, camels and people would be there and the many other things we had heard about but never seen. We talked about the sea, the rivers, castles, trains, toyshops, fruit trees, candy and ice cream shops, football games and everything else that village children imagine there to be in the big city. There were no newspapers, magazines, TVs or radios in the village to give us an idea of life in Beirut. The stories we had heard from our parents or others who had been to Beirut quickly began to take on a life of their own as we boys talked, and exhausted ourselves with our fantasies.

The excitement lasted for a few days and then things quieted down and returned to normal. However, Sabih had brought with him a used soccer ball from Beirut and gave it to me and cautioned me not to play with it on the street and not to lose it either. A few days later, my friends and I were playing with the ball on the street when suddenly the town policeman showed up and took the ball away and told me that he would give it to my father. I got perturbed and pleaded meekly with the policeman to return the ball to me and promised not to play on the street again. Farid, the policeman, did not budge until he saw a group of three young, sophisticated college girls from Beirut walking by in their colourful shorts. Farid nonchalantly called me and told me he would return the ball to me, provided I would grab a branch from the nearby mulberry tree and stick the branch between the legs of the blond girl in the group. Without any hesitation, I grabbed a branch from the mulberry tree and sneaked slowly behind the girls and was about to stick the branch between the blond girl's legs when my mother appeared suddenly, on her way to visit a friend. I dropped the branch right there and then and fled away. In the evening, I was taking a bath and called my mother to rub my back. She did, but proceeded to lecture me and ended up with slapping my buttocks a few times for my mischievous behaviour that same day. I got mad and ran away naked and hid in a bush two blocks away. Half an hour later, my dad was returning home and saw me in the bush and asked me what was the matter, while he was wrapping me up in his coat. After I explained between sniffles and tears, my dad broke into loud laughter and I joined in a little later as we walked home together.

It was time for me to get ready to leave to school. As the preparations began, my spirits sank and I became hesitant about what to pack and how to prepare. Finally, after a few days of getting my things together, it was time to say good-bye to my parents, my sisters and brother, my friends and all the neighbours. Every one gathered at our house on the Friday evening to give advice and wish me well. I was warned repeatedly not to pick up the city accent and manners, which were so much abhorred by the village people. Eventually my mother had to send everyone home as it was getting late and I would have to be up early to catch the bus to Beirut.

I did not sleep well, and was up soon after the first call of the rooster. The whole family got up soon after for a final breakfast together. My father packed up the sleeping mattress and my mother finished packing my clothes in a large hamper. The mattress was rolled up, wrapped in burlap and tied firmly with a rope to prevent it from unfurling. I kissed my mother, sisters and brother good-bye and, grabbing my hamper, followed my father, who was carrying the bedroll, down the street to the bus stop. Several villagers were already waiting at the bus stop. All of them knew I was heading to Beirut to attend school and they began to wish me well. Michel, however, took the opportunity to tease me, saying there would be no more hills and trees to climb and no friends to play with.

I could hear the bus horn long before the bus came into sight. I watched excitedly as the driver pulled the bus to a stop and descended to help his assistant load the luggage onto the roof of the bus. Soon, the driver waved his waiting passengers onto the bus, making a point of keeping the front seats clear for my father and me, so I could have the best view of Beirut as we drove into the city. The road down to Beirut was steep and winding and would pass through numerous villages and towns, each one producing more passengers until the bus was uncomfortably full. It was a ten-mile trip from the village to the sea and the outskirts of Beirut. It was only after the bus had traveled through the village of Bikfaya, at around 3000 feet above sea level that Beirut finally came into view. It was a magnificent sight: buildings of all shapes and sizes whose chimneys spewed smoke in all shapes and colours, the brilliant blue sea segueing into the clear blue sky, a sunrise sparkling as though its rays were made of diamond and gold strings, ships and boats appeared to be scattered haphazardly between sea and sky, lush groves of trees and beds of colourful flowers, everything blanketed with the hum of human activity, and the songs and voices of birds and animals that shared the city with its people. This was the vision of Beirut imprinted in my mind upon seeing the city for the first time. Unconsciously, I let out a gasp. I turned to my father and exclaimed: "What a beautiful city!" Other passengers heard my excitement and turned to look at the city as though for the first time. The short silence was broken by the sound of a woman singing, asking the sea why her loved ones had been taken away, and not yet returned, for they had promised they would return. One by one, the passengers joined in, except me since I had not heard that song before. My father leaned over and explained that the singer was lamenting the emigration of her husband and two of her children to the USA, even while she was on her way to the bank in Beirut to cash a cheque recently arrived from her husband. The bus driver, Adib, added that it was not unusual for this woman to sing the same song each time she rode to Beirut to cash her cheques. She had a beautiful voice and the passengers always enjoyed her singing.

I had heard Beirut described as a giant holding back the sea with its two arms, as though to prevent the waters from swallowing the buildings that lined the shore in a semicircle. There were no obvious spaces between the buildings, which appeared crowded together like a crush of shoppers at a farmers' market. In comparison, the outskirts of the city were green and buildings dotted the greenery like a sparse design woven into a carpet. The early morning sun hit the sea at an angle, setting off sparkles that hurt the viewer's eyes. As the bus approached the city, I could see that the sea was choppy, white-capped waves cascading into the shore. The moored ships loomed over the private sailboats anchored nearby. The colour of the sea changed as it neared the shore, to a dark blue flecked with grey. The colours of the buildings became more distinct as the bus drove nearer the city. Most were dark grey, most with faded red tiles covering the roofs. I could see a mass of white clouds on the horizon; they appeared to be on the run from the warm rays of the sun.

The bus had arrived at the seashore by the time the woman at the back of the bus had finished singing her lament. At this level, I could see that the shoreline soon ran into an expanse of inland plains, covered with orchards of oranges, lemons, bananas, and palm trees as well as fields of sugar canes and pomegranate shrubs. On both sides of the road were vegetable and fruit stands, with more people engaged in commerce than I had ever seen. My heart was throbbing with excitement; I could hardly believe I was truly awake and not dreaming. I now realized that my fantasies of what Beirut would be like had fallen far short of the reality. I turned to my father and began to pester him with questions. "Why don't we have fields and orchards like these in Shweir?" "Who would buy all that food? It could feed thousands!" My father patiently explained that these trees I was now seeing could not survive without the moderate climate and access to water from the rivers that ran in Beirut. And merchants from Beirut and surrounding towns and villages would buy the produce to sell in their stores.

When we had arrived at the city outskirts, the bus driver turned and asked me to close the window I had been leaning out of, to prevent flies from entering the bus and bothering the rest of the passengers. I did as I was asked but it was already too late. A number of flies had already flown in. I was astonished at their size and colour. They seemed to be at least twice as large as the flies I was used to seeing in the village. I watched the flies buzz around the interior of the bus for a minute or two, but soon turned back to staring out the window. I was again quickly absorbed in the passing scenes. The bus drove down a road lined with massive willow trees whose branches met above the road to form a leafy green arch. The arch was not solid enough to block out the sun, however, and the road was bathed with dancing specks of light.

The bus exited the tunnel of leaves and light and soon crossed a bridge that spanned the main city river. The riverbed was dry, with only a thin stream of water running down the center. I asked my father in astonishment if this was the same mighty river I had studied about in my geography class. My father answered in the affirmative, but hastened to add that it was a dry year and the river water had been depleted by the need to irrigate the city's orchards. On the other side of the river, traffic had slowed to a halt. I stared in fascination at the long line of cars, trucks, buses, carts, people, donkeys, camels and goats that filled the road ahead of our bus, all apparently trying to squeeze closer together than they already were. The bus driver told me to look straight ahead where I would soon see a train cross the road. Soon after, we heard the whistle of the train as it approached from the left. The sound became louder by the second and as the bus passengers turned in the direction of the sound they could see the accompanying billows of smoke. Within seconds, the train itself appeared, massive and noisy, causing the donkeys to bray, the goats to jump and the watching people to cheer. I stared open mouthed at the first train I had ever seen. I had never imagined it could be so long and each car so large, almost three times larger than the bus I was sitting in. The train was loaded with cars of coal, timber, sheep, steel, grain and even motor vehicles. As the last train car disappeared to the right, the traffic began to slowly move again. I watched a flock of goats with particular interest. As their herder moved the goats forward, they were picking up garbage and all kinds of peels from the side of the road and munching on their finds. As I watched, a woman appeared at the door of an apartment building on the side of the street; she held a jug in her right hand, which she held up and waved at the goat herder. When the goat herder spotted the jug, he stopped his flock and took the jug from the woman. The herder knelt down to milk one of his skinny goats, filling the jug with warm milk. Once the jug was full, he returned it to the woman, who gave him some coins in exchange. The goat herder then raised his stick and prodded his puck, the lead goat, which started forward with a tinkle of his bell, the rest of the flock soon following. As the bus pulled away, I could hear the goat herder singing out in a loud, clear voice that he had fresh milk for sale.

Suddenly, a trolley car appeared on the right. The conductor was sounding the bell and traffic once again came to a halt to allow the trolley to roll forward on its tracks into the main road. I watched wide-eyed as a young man jumped off the slowly moving trolley and others, previously standing on the street, grabbed hold and jumped on. I was thrilled with the daring of the young men, for their actions looked very dangerous to me. I had begun to imagine myself doing the same challenging action when the bus driver interrupted my thought and told me not to learn these tricks as he knew of one man who had tumbled off the trolley and had his arm run over by the same car he had fallen from. His arm had been amputated. I was not sure I believed the story but several passengers sitting nearby said that they too had heard about the incident and one said he had seen it happen. This was enough to convince me and I swore never to take such chances on the tramway.

The effect on me of all the different sights and sounds, combined with the change in atmospheric pressure that had already blocked my ears, was oppressive. The bus driver noticed this change in me and began to tease me that perhaps I should have stayed home to play with my friends instead of coming to Beirut with its crowded streets and depressing atmosphere. The driver had accurately read my mind, but I kept quiet and held back the tears forming in my eyes. I was determined not to embarrass my father or myself; my father was looking at me to gauge my reaction to the bus driver's teasing. With a firm voice, my father interrupted the bus driver's chatter to say that the school was really quite nice and I would be too busy studying to have time to wander through the dirty, busy streets of Beirut.

It was not long after hearing my father's voice and reassuring words that I realized the bus driver had pulled over to the side of the road and indicated that we had arrived at our destination. My father paid the driver and gathered up our luggage. Once my father and I had left the bus, we stood back to watch it work its way back into the traffic. Then, my father led the way up the sharply climbing street, carrying my bedroll and clothes, and I followed with the food hamper. The street was not as crowded as some I had observed from the bus. There were candy, ice cream, halva, cookies and toyshops on both sides of the street and the sweet smells caused me to swallow involuntarily several times. My blocked ears soon opened from my swallowing and the street sounds flooded in more clearly than ever before.

Soon, the street began to seem a little longer and the food

hamper a little heavier than when we had got off the bus. I was relieved when my father asked me if I wanted an ice cream and we soon stopped by one of the street cart vendors. I found the vanilla ice cream to be delicious beyond my wildest expectations and could easily have eaten a few more, but I did not dare ask my father for another. We soon resumed our climb up the street, eventually turning left onto a narrow, dirt footpath.

"Your uncle's apartment is at the end of this path," said my father, with relief in his voice.

I felt my heart beat faster and my stomach tighten excitedly. My eyes focused intently on the end of the path and I did not notice that I was walking between tall apartment buildings, lemon, orange, palm, and banana trees, all at once. It was only later that I discovered the trees and learned that they were all that was left from the original farmland that had been subdivided to make room for the apartment buildings. While I trudged forward toward the ancient building at the end of the footpath, I could hear birds singing, as though to welcome me to the neighbourhood.

The two-storey building I walked towards was built of sandstones, with a large stained wooden door in the middle of the front wall and two large rectangular glass paned windows on either side of the door. As we approached, I could see that the side walls each had five large windows, identical to those on the front of the house. The house was about one hundred years old and in a state of mild disrepair. The walls and windows looked like they had not been painted or repaired in years.

My father pointed to the first window on the left of the front door and said, "That is your uncle's apartment."

I got excited and very happy as I began to make out my grandmother waving at me through the window. She then suddenly disappeared from the window. Despite my tiredness and the weight of the food hamper, I began to run towards the front door. As I approached, the front door swung wide open and my grandmother Nabiha stood there, her arms open. She hugged and kissed my father and me and ushered us from the long, wide hall into her own apartment. Out of the corner of my eye, I noticed that each side of the marble hallway sported five large doors, separated from each other by about 16 feet. My grandmother, Imm Sabih, explained that each door led into another apartment, except the last door on the left which lead into a large common kitchen and two bathrooms, shared by all the residents, about 60 people altogether. Between four and seven people lived in each apartment. Fortunately, at least twelve of the residents worked shift work, and sharing the bathrooms could be accomplished without too much jostling. Nevertheless, sometimes the line in front of the bathrooms would snake down the hallway and the marble space would ring with gossip and laughter. Although the kitchen appeared spacious when empty, there were usually between nine and twelve people jostling for room in there at any one time. The odours and the aroma of food emanating from the kitchen nearly knocked me off my feet the first time I ventured to that end of the hallway.

In my grandmother's apartment, I noted two neatly made metal beds, one in each of the back corners. There was also a dining table with five chairs, a shelf groaning under jars of spices, pink pickled turnips, jam and molasses. Small bags of rice, lentil, chickpeas, and white peas were on a lower shelf. In a third corner, were a chair and a sofa, which could be converted into a bed. Three pots with nice beautiful flowers were squeezed together in the fourth corner of the neat apartment. The two large windows were covered with mobile wooden shutters on the outside and cloth drapes on the inside. The one-room apartment was very clean and tidy and it felt immediately comfortable to me.

Once my father and I had put down our loads, Sitto Imm Sabih hugged and kissed me warmly again and nearly cried with happiness at having us with her. She then handed my father a towel and lead us down to the washbasin in the kitchen where we could wash our faces and freshen up from our trip. Once my father and I had returned to the small apartment by the front door, Sitto once again hugged me and kissed me and served us fresh squeezed lemonade. I was too excited to sit still and visit with my father and grandmother and asked if I could go out and see the neighbourhood and my new school.

"Not just yet," said my grandmother, "even adults get lost in this neighbourhood because the streets and buildings all look so similar. Why don't you play in the front courtyard for now and we'll all go out for a tour once your uncle gets home from work."

Temporarily satisfied with this explanation, I ran out to explore the front courtyard. I found a massive walnut tree and several orange and lemon trees that were heavy with green fruit. I began to imagine building a tree house in the top leafy branches of the walnut tree from where I could reach and eat the ripened fruit of the orange trees. The chicken coop in the far corner held my grandma's chicken and inspired yet another fantasy, this one of fresh eggs for breakfast. I eyed the fence surrounding the courtyard, which was built of rubble masonry. I ran my hands over it to test for footholds, but the mortar layer on top of the fence, studded with broken glass, quickly brought an end to my visions of leaping over the fence. I did not like the fence, thinking it would prevent me from playing with any children my age living next door. I was pondering what to do about it when my thoughts were interrupted by the singsong chanting of a produce salesman peddling his goods from a wooden cart he pushed ahead of him into the courtyard. The neighbourhood women began to gather in the courtyard, Sitto Imm Sabih among them. She motioned to me to come to her so that she could introduce me to her neighbours and to Halim, the produce salesman.

With a twinkle in his eye, Halim said to me, "You better study hard and do well at school or you will end up competing with me and working like a dog to make a living."

Mrs. Karam, who lived in the apartment next door to Sitto, retorted, "With the prices you charge, Halim, you'll soon be able to buy the building out from under us and you'd probably raise the rent to boot!"

Once the laughter had died down, I announced that I wanted to become a doctor or an engineer so that I could help my parents, my family and the people in my village.

"Good for you, Karim," remarked Mrs. Sawaya, "You're a good boy and you'll be in school with my son George."

I perked up at hearing this and asked where George was, thinking I had found a playmate.

"George has gone to school with his father," began Mrs. Sawaya, but Mrs. Touma interrupted her and pointed at George and his father coming down the alley. As the group looked over at George, he broke into a run and skidded to a stop in front of his mother, to announce in a loud, excited voice that he had registered but he had to go back that afternoon to buy his books. I was surprised to recognize George's father as the teacher whom I had met at my Jiddo's funeral and made haste to present myself to Mikhail, who recognized me and greeted me warmly.

"If you are ready right after lunch you can come with me and George to school to register," said Mikhail. I grinned and said I would just have to check with my father before agreeing. About an hour later, with permission granted and lunch eaten, I skipped out into the courtyard to meet George and his father and the three of us set off for the school, George and I walking a few yards ahead of Mikhail. I drew back at the first street we were to cross as there were no sidewalks and pedestrians were scrambling from building entrance to open staircase to alley-ways to avoid being hit by the cars speeding down the street. The street was lined with tall buildings, which prevented the sun from reaching the street. It was the worst part of the walk to school. Once we had crossed the street and turned down a corner, the rest of the walk was on a wide street with sidewalks. We paused outside a small store while Mikhail went in to buy a package of cigarettes. George pointed out that the store sold candy and lemonade and was a restaurant, too. He then pointed out each small, specialized business which lined the street, the grocery store, the butcher shop, the flower shop, the bookstore, the shoe store, the clothes store, a bakery and more. Mikhail came out of the restaurant and interrupted the tour by handing each one of us a chocolate bar. We thanked Mr. Sawaya and unwrapped our treats, dropping the wrapping on the sidewalk, as was the habit of most people in Beirut. The streets were littered with garbage. The street cleaners had their work cut out for them.

When we arrived at the school, Mikhail led us to the director's office where I completed the forms to register for grade four. The director welcomed me and handed me a list of books and supplies I would need to purchase from the school's bookstore. As there was a large crowd in front of the bookstore, George took me on a quick tour of the classrooms and the playgrounds. All looked clean and large compared to the one-room school I had attended in my village. I could see equipment for volleyball and gymnastics and asked how I could get on the volleyball team.

"I am on the team and we'll need players," said George. "Final selection will be in about two weeks."

After hearing that good news, I suggested that we go back to the bookstore and purchase books according to the list I had. With that done, George, his father and I walked back to the apartment.

I was very happy to see my Uncle Sabih and my aunts Marie and Badre, who had all returned home from work, sitting in the apartment with my father and my grandmother. I told them about my day and that I was now registered and had purchased my books and supplies. My father, pleased that everything we had planned had been accomplished, then said it was time for him to return to the village, Shweir. After some coffee, cakes and more talk, my father gathered up a few things and stood at the door to say good-bye. I felt my spirits sink heavily as I hugged and said good-bye to my father, but soon the excitement of the day, the pleasure my Grandma and her family took in my presence and the prospect of beginning school the next day, dispelled the sadness at saying good-bye to my father. I was settling in for the long haul.

Shortly after my father left to return to Shweir, George appeared at the door to ask if I wanted to play soccer with some of the neighbourhood boys. I turned back into the apartment to get my Uncle's permission, and once I had it, ran out into the courtyard with George to meet the other players. The game was played in the alley-way in front of the apartment building as there were no playgrounds nearby and the building courtyard was too small for the game. There was lots of excitement and shouting as the game got underway, and the boys put on their best style to impress me, the new kid on the block. Only when George kicked a high ball that crashed through Imm Khalil's window did the game break up, the players scattering in all directions. Imm Khalil stormed out the main door of her apartment building, shouting and demanding to know who had broken her window. She spotted George and me running into our own building and followed us into the hallway, still shouting. As George tried to explain to his father what had happened, the other building residents began to stream out of their apartments into the hallway to see what was causing the commotion and to contribute their own ideas on what to do next.

3

School Excursions to Sidon and Baalbek

I did well at the tryouts for the school volleyball team and was chosen to play next to the team captain. I vowed to practice regularly and to contribute to the success of the team. On the way home that day, I played pass with one of my new schoolmates, Jamil. As we neared the main street, the ball slipped from Jamil's hand and rolled onto the street. Jamil began to run after the ball without checking for cars. I yelled at him to stop, as I had seen a car speeding towards us, but Jamil ignored the warning, probably relying on the accepted principle that pedestrians have the right of way. There was a horrible thud as Jamil was hit by the speeding vehicle and thrown off his feet, into the air and smack into a light post. The driver of the car did not stop, leaving Jamil lying on the side of the street and I in a panic. Jamil moaned and brought his hand to his throat, which was badly lacerated. Luckily, one of the neighbours had seen the accident and ran over to gather Jamil up and drive him to the hospital. I watched silently as Jamil was bundled up and placed in the neighbour's car. The car roared off and I was left standing by the side of the street; I picked up the tennis ball, which had come to a rest by the curb, and resumed my walk home in a sad state.

I was subdued when I arrived home and Uncle Sabih asked me what was the matter. I hesitated at first, but finally told my Uncle what had happened. Sabih understood my sadness but repeated his standard lecture about never playing on the street and watching constantly and carefully for traffic. He reminded me that I no longer lived in a small quiet mountain village and that I now had to watch out constantly for traffic of all kinds. I would have to be careful to stay out of the way of cars, trucks, donkeys, mules and all kinds of carts that were competing for space on the narrow streets of Beirut.

Later that evening, Sabih took me to inquire about Jamil. We discovered that Jamil's larynx had been badly hurt and he was not allowed to talk. Jamil's mother, who was sitting by his bedside, told Sabih and me that there was a 50/50 chance Jamil would never fully recover his voice. As we walked home after our visit, Sabih again sternly reminded me never to play on the street. I remained sitting quietly in the apartment for the rest of the evening and then went to bed early, to avoid any further discussion of the day's events with the curious neighbours.

I soon settled into the routines of school, using any free time I had to practice volleyball. I heard that the school had an annual trip to Sidon to tour the historic castles from the era of the Crusaders and to compete in a volleyball tournament with the Freres School in Sidon. On the day of the trip to Sidon, three buses were hired and the boys reported to school at 6:00 AM. It took 25 minutes to corral the excited boys into their designated seats and the buses finally chugged out of the schoolyard at 6:30. The students were noisy and excited and the only way to channel their energy was to get them singing a medley of school, national and religious songs which we kept up for the 90-minute trip south to Sidon. The road we traveled ran parallel to the seashore, and meandered through groves of orange, banana, olive, pine, loquat and other fruit trees. We passed through tiny fishing villages and vegetable garden towns where the village wares were displayed in the covered huts by the sides of the road. Many farmers built branch-covered huts by the sides of their homes in which to display their wares. This agricultural strip appeared to extend one mile inland, after which I could see rising, rolling hills, covered with groves of trees.

Shortly after the bus had left the outskirts of Beirut, Mr. Mikhail had stood up at the front of the bus and demanded quiet from the boys for an announcement. After taking a deep breath and puffing his chest, he told the still wriggling boys that within a few minutes we would pass the beach area of Khaldeh where two steel towers had recently been erected for the new Lebanese radio station. He explained to us about radio waves and how the towers were constructed out of steel rods and guy wires and went on to boast that the Khaldeh towers had been erected by technicians from the town of Shweir, his hometown, as well as that of several of the other boys on the bus.

As soon as Mr. Mikhail had finished speaking, a young, high and squeaky voice sang out from the back of the bus:

"I come from the invincible village of Shweir,
Its men built the highest Khaldeh towers in the world."

The rest of the boys on the bus soon joined in and their voices filled the bus for the chorus:

"Three cheers for the invincible village of Shweir."

A few minutes later, Mr. Mikhail stood up again to make a second announcement, this time explaining that the bus would soon pass through the banana orchards and the village of Damur.

The same squeaky voice that had started the song for Shweir now blurted out, "Damuri bananas are the favourite of Emir Bechir!" The Emir was a prince and had been the ruler of Lebanon in the late 1800s.

On hearing this, Eli Matni and Anwar, a student from Shweir, demanded that the bus stop and they be allowed to taste the bananas from the orchard of Eli Matni's parents. Mr. Mikhail laughed along with the boys and asked the bus driver to stop for half an hour in the farmers' market; the students could stretch their legs and buy some bananas if they wanted. Eli, Anwar and a few other boys treated themselves to the ripe, yellow, speckled bananas from the Matni's stand, while the rest of the students milled about and bought bananas from nearby vendors. Eli's mother was manning the stand and was overjoyed to see her son. She gave him a loving hug and wished him luck in the tournament. The boys were soon called back to the bus and their journey resumed. After a few minutes, the bus came to a narrow bridge several centuries old, which crossed the Damur River. Only one vehicle could pass over the bridge at a time and the drivers on either side were supposed to give the right of way to whoever first reached the edge of the bridge. That morning, a convoy of mules and bugles, loaded with bananas, was slowly crossing the bridge, bringing traffic on either side to a halt. My schoolmates and I were fascinated with the traffic jam and thrilled at hearing the shouting and honking that was taking place at both ends of the bridge.

Mr. Mikhail took the opportunity to point out to his charges that the bridge was built of three masonry arches that dated back to the Roman Empire and spanned a narrow, high gorge. The bridge abutments looked extremely tall and slender and not particularly safe, yet they had withstood the ravages of time and the weight of the invading armies that had regularly crossed back and forth over the bridge for several centuries. Eventually, the school buses made their way across the bridge and drove onto another, much more dilapidated bridge, which stood at the mouth of the Awwali River on the edge of the city of Sidon. Here, the river was much wider and the bridge was built on twelve short masonry arches that settled in the sand of the riverbed. Willow trees lined the riverbanks and the road followed a long, wide beach of white sand toward the city entrance. As the bus approached the river, Mr. Mikhail instructed the boys to look for the Crusaders' castle on the right hand side of the road. A long wide ramp led to the castle ruins, which jutted some distance into the Mediterranean Sea. Mr. Mikhail explained that the castle had been abandoned centuries ago and remained abandoned to this day. He also explained that "Awwali", in Arabic, means the "first river" but that some claimed the word was a distortion of the French Crusaders' description of the river as being "comme lait," like milk. This story delighted the boys and they responded by singing and shouting back and forth to each other "cherchez le lait!"

The walled city of Sidon can be entered from one of three city gates, but the school buses and even cars were too big to drive through the gates. The drivers parked their buses outside the city walls, near the "Fawqa" (upper) gate, which was also near the Freres School where the volleyball tournament was to be held. The Moslem cemetery was also located near the Fawqa gate and as we boys were descending from the buses, we noticed a funeral procession winding its way toward the cemetery. Mr. Mikhail hushed us and reminded us sternly to keep quiet and show respect for the deceased. Jamil and I were still on the bus and could clearly see the procession from our higher perch. We watched the Sheik lead the funeral procession in prayer. The body was wrapped tightly in a white cloth and a "tarbooch" hat was pinned to one end of the coffin. Four well-built men dressed in black were carrying the body on a flat wooden coffin. The procession moved quickly and soon passed through the cemetery gates. After the Sheik said the last prayer the wrapped body was placed in a recently dug burial hole underground. The mourners then filed out of the cemetery gates on their way to the deceased's home.

Mr. Mikhail gathered us boys together and began to issue instructions. He cautioned us to stay close together and follow him to the school. He pointed out that the streets were packed with people, animals and carts and it would be very easy to get separated and lost if we didn't pay attention and follow his instructions. With that, Mr. Mikhail turned and led us through the city gate.

As I passed through the gate, the misty aroma that I soon learned was unique to Sidon overwhelmed most of the students and me. I breathed in hesitantly to fill my lungs with the warm, moist air produced by the restaurants, wholesale and retail outlets, processing candy plants, donkeys, dogs, cats, fish, and people packed into the covered, winding streets. The smells floated on the thick underlying sea air. After the initial shock of the all encompassing stuffy air, I felt soothed by it as we squeezed our way through the milling crowds. I was surprised to discover that I could separate the aromas from each other and actually recognize their original source. The covered streets were poorly lit except for the occasional shop front whose light bulbs had been strung on a rope to attract customers. I was attracted by one well-lit halvah shop, where the sweet was being produced in front of an open window, and its delicious sugary aroma attracted many customers to watch the display and purchase small portions for a snack. We were fascinated by the many small shops and the masses of displayed merchandise and were hard-pressed to keep our eyes on the teacher.

Eventually, we arrived, miraculously all together, at the Freres school. We found the Freres' senior and junior volleyball teams already warming up in the courtyard, awaiting our arrival. Greetings were exchanged all around and after an initial period of warm up for our boys from St. Sauveur, the competition began on two separate courts, one for the senior team and one for the junior team. There were plenty of spectators and their cheering encouraged the teams. After a morning of competition, the St. Sauveur junior team had lost but the senior team was spurred to victory by an exceptional performance by Anis, its captain. When the competition was finished, we were sent off to buy our lunch from the nearby restaurants and street kiosks. Most of us opted for falafel, shawarma, fish and halvah. After lunch, the instructors led us on a tour of the Crusaders' castle, the "kalah". The kalah was in ruins, huge but finished boulders strewn around in no particular order, but forming the vaguely recognizable outline of a castle which used to jut into the sea and serve as a protective quay for the harbour. We could see a few fishermen squatting here and there on the boulders, repairing their nets or carrying out other routine chores prior to beginning their daily fishing routine.

After the tour of kalah, we moved on as a group to view a famous café located in the main courtyard of the old city of Sidon. To get to the café, we had to work our way through a maze of narrow, covered streets. When we walked out into the courtyard, it was with a feeling of relief to see the blue sky, the large tree in the centre of the courtyard and the splashing fountain. The edge of the courtyard was lined with several cafes, each with its own outdoor tables and potted flowers and plants. Many of the tables were occupied with men playing cards, dominoes or backgammon and drinking coffee, tea or lemonade. Many of the men were smoking cigarettes or puffing on the "arkyle", also called the hubbly bubbly or hookah. The objective of our visit was the famous "hakawaty", or storyteller who daily, at 3:00 PM, in one of the cafes, told tales of the heroic acts of Antar and his wife, Ablah, two well-known

Arab folk heroes. We found seats inside the café and ordered drinks of lemonade, coffee and tea and waited for the storyteller to appear. Only three kerosene lamps lit the interior of the café. Through the murky light, I watched as the head waiter climbed onto a small platform at the back of the café. The waiter, dressed in black garb and a white shirt, began to beat a drum to attract the attention of the customers. The café gradually quieted down, until the only sound to be heard was the throbbing of the drum. The waiter then put down the drum and, after a few words of welcome, introduced the hakawaty, Mohamed, who today would be describing Antar leading the battle to secure the Qaisumah oasis for his tribe.

In captivating detail, Mohamed described how Antar captured the Sheik of the Obeyed tribe and held him prisoner. We were enthralled and listened intently to the exciting description. After thirty minutes, Mohamed drew his story to a close and invited the crowd to return again tomorrow to discover the fate of Sheik Obeyed. My classmates jumped up and gave Mohamed a standing ovation for his rousing oratory and begged to hear more today as we would be back in Beirut tomorrow. Mohamed smiled at our enthusiasm, but could not be convinced to carry on. We then had to follow our instructors back to the buses for the drive back to Beirut, but we continued to create our own stories about Antar and to speculate on what Mohamed would be telling his audience the next day. The only stop on the way back was halfway home, at the town of Jiyeh, to buy a snack of Romaine lettuce. By 6:00 PM, the buses had arrived back at the school in Beirut and we were sent home.

The next day, the school routine returned to normal, although we continued to create and play out scenarios from the life of Antar and Ablah, holding mock battles and taking each other prisoner during the morning and lunch breaks. A few days later, in a religion class, we were told that we would be going to a movie theatre five minutes from the school to see a movie about the crucifixion of Jesus. The Moslem and the Jewish students were given the option of joining their classmates to see the movie or to take the afternoon off. After lunch, we were lined up in pairs and five teachers escorted us through the narrow city streets to the theatre. Eli, Mohamed, a Moslem classmate and I were walking towards the playground arguing about some of the details of crucifixion, which we were hoping the movie would clear up. Mohamed, although a Moslem, was attending the Greek Catholic school in order to learn about Christianity. His father was a politician, married to a Christian woman, and if Mohamed was to follow in his footsteps, as his parents expected, he would have to learn about the traditions of all the various religious sects found in Lebanon so that he would be aware and knowledgeable about the beliefs and traditions of his constituents.

The movie about the crucifixion turned out to be powerful and emotional. Most of the students and I cried loudly when Christ was crucified, and then we were elated when he rose from the dead and ascended to heaven. As we returned to school after the movie, Mohamed pestered Eli and me with questions about the birth of Christ, his baptism and his ability to feed a large crowd with five loaves of bread and two fishes. Eli was in the middle of expounding on the meaning of the miracles when he was interrupted by a man on the other side of the street calling to Mohamed to remind him to come the next day to the racetrack a half hour early. Mohamed waved and called halo to Nassib, who was a horse trainer, and asked if he could bring his two friends, Eli and Karim, with him. Nassib responded gruffly, "Two friends only, no more." Mohamed cried out with excitement and quickly turned to ask Eli and me if we would like to come with him to the racetrack tomorrow to watch the horse races.

"Of course," we said in unison, and quickly dropped our religious discussion to work out the details of where, when and how the three of us would be let in through a back door at the racetrack, used only by the trainers.

The next day, we three boys met at the school at 12:30 and after some preliminary tussling around, we began to make our way to the racetrack. We took the electric train, which cost each of us five piastres (cents). The train we took happened to have a musically talented conductor who was ringing the train's bell to the tune of the "Battle Hymn" and rolling his train to the same beat. We sat quickly in the second-class section on hard wooden benches and grabbed the steel bar railings to stay put and avoid swaying with the speeding train. Mohamed pointed out certain landmarks to us while the train clacked down the tracks. This was the first time I rode the train and ventured into a new part of the city and Mohamed pointed out various large buildings to fascinate me. We passed the Lycee, a non-religious school for boys, the St. Paul College of Medicine, the Jewish cemetery, a public fountain and a French armory.

Eventually, we reached the new Lebanese museum of antiquities at the edge of the pine forest where the racetrack was located. We got off the train at the museum station and began to follow a short trail through a thick forest, which led us to the rear entrance of the racetrack where Nassib had said he would meet us. The forest was filled with fairly old pine trees which thrived in a red sandy soil. They had been planted there to prevent the wind from eroding the southern outskirts of Beirut. We found Nassib waiting for us and with a smile he asked us to follow him. Nassib led us to a spot near the fence that surrounded the track. There were a few other horse trainers there who were sitting in a shaded area on wooden benches. The view of the track was exceptionally good and Nassib was treating us with great warmth and friendliness.

The first race got under way at 2:00 PM. The horses thundered past to the shouted encouragement of the crowd and the sounds of the track soon worked to increase our excitement. Nassib left us to ourselves as one of his horses was scheduled to run in the last scheduled race, which also had the biggest prize. As the afternoon wore on, the noise and excitement began to wear us down and it was with a little relief that we heard the last race announced at 4:30. Nassib's horse, El Bark, the lightning, was in fifth place after the first lap. El Bark was a crowd favourite and the shouts and encouragement for El Bark to move ahead became deafening. The effect on El Bark was like magic and his pace picked up until he began to pass in turn each of the four horses that were ahead of him. The noise of the crowd reached a fever pitch in response and El Bark kept responding by running even faster. He miraculously won the race by two full lengths.

Mohamed, Eli and I felt a surge of pride as we watched El Bark being led into the winner's circle by his owner, Mr. Sursock, the jockey, Abed, and Nassib. Mr. Sursock was presented with a trophy and the prize as the spectators roared, clapped and shouted: "El Bark is the champion, three cheers for El Bark and Mr. Sursock." Once the winning ceremonies were over, Nassib led El Bark to the area where we the three boys and the other trainers were waiting. The trainers broke into a ribald congratulatory song, revised for the occasion to recognize the winner:

> I wish I were a horse
> In Mr. Sursock's stable
> I would eat peanuts
> Drink fresh lemonade
> And pass out hazelnuts!

We were allowed to pet El Bark after we had congratulated Nassib on the win. Nassib gave us barbecued almonds and sent us on our way home as the supper hour was fast approaching and he wanted to celebrate with his friends.

My move to Beirut was proving to be a source of much excitement for me and school was the source of many new things. A few days after my two friends and I had spent the afternoon at the race track, our history teacher, Mr. Akkawi, told the class we would soon be going on a trip to visit the ruins of the Baalbek temples, once we had finished reading the chapter on the Roman Empire. The promise of a road trip inspired us to promise to complete the reading within the next two weeks. We were studying the history and the influence of the Greeks and the Romans on the Middle East. Baal was the Roman god of the Sun and the temples had been erected in his honour in the Beka' valley, long considered the granary of the Roman Empire. With the field trip as our goal, the class quickly got through our reading and handed in our written assignments on Monday, within the set deadline. The field trip was then scheduled for the following Thursday and we were told to meet at the school at 4:30 AM, to allow time for the buses to drive to Baalbek. The morning of the trip, I got to school on time, as did all the other boys in my class, except Eli. I watched with interest as Mr. Akkawi, paced up and down the front of the school, muttering to himself about Eli's tardiness and slowly working himself into a temper. Luckily, when Eli finally came running up, he offered enough apologies and promises to defuse Mr. Akkawi's temper and the school trip soon got on the road without mishap. We were kept strictly in line and not a peep was allowed while the bus driver concentrated on driving through the narrow streets of Beirut. Once the bus had reached the city outskirts, the driver visibly relaxed and Mr. Akkawi, who had been sitting directly behind the driver and watching intently, turned and gave us permission to talk and even sing if we wanted, as long as we stayed seated. The noise soon became deafening as different groups of friends tried to drown out others and Mr. Akkawi was forced once again to take control. He chose to let us sing but in unison, mainly songs from the school repertoire.

Soon after the bus left the outskirts of Beirut, it began to climb a steep mountain road. The pitch of this road was so steep at one point that the driver pulled the bus over to the side of the road and Mr. Akkawi asked us to get off the bus so that the driver could negotiate a particularly steep and narrow curve. This caused even more excitement and Mr. Akkawi was hard pressed to keep us in line and then get us back on the bus so the journey could continue. The road passed through many villages, and the countryside was alternately bare and well-treed. Eventually, the road narrowed to a passageway that was a little less than nine feet wide and it was this passageway that led to the Beka' valley. From that point on, the road was downhill and my fellow travelers and I could see the entire Beka' valley in one vista. It was a breath-taking sight, and appeared to me to be as beautiful as a rich Persian carpet, covered with alternating patches of green, gold and brown, and studded with small villages and stands of trees. As the bus continued to drive deeper into the valley, we spotted a roadside watermelon stand and with one voice beseeched our teacher and the driver to pull over and allow us to quench our thirst. As Mr. Akkawi was thirsty, too, and the driver felt like he needed a break, they were easily convinced to stop for the fresh watermelon, which turned out to be wonderfully sweet and juicy. A nearby pasture held a few cows, donkeys and horses, and soon each one of the animals had worked their way over to the side of the pasture fence to inspect us and beg for handouts. They were amply rewarded, as we were eager to feed the animals the watermelon rinds.

Once Mr. Akkawi had corralled us back onto the bus, we continued our journey into the valley. The Beka' valley is long, narrow and flat and cultivated with fields of wheat, barley, corn, watermelon, cucumber and other vegetables that thrive in a semi-moist environment. Only a few of the farms needed to be irrigated from artesian wells. Many small villages dotted the valley and were easily spotted by the smoke rising from the chimneys of the village houses. The road ran almost straight through the valley, passing through the lush fields of grains and vegetables. Away from the main road, some farmers were known to grow poppy plants for export and for local consumption. That morning, the sun was shining brightly with only the odd, fat white cloud puffing across the sky in no particular direction. A light mist rose from the fields, as though lazily trying to reach up and embrace the sun's rays. The bus was quiet as we were lulled to sleep by the monotonous humming of the engine and the warmth of the sun. After another hour of driving, with the majority of the boys and Mr. Akkawi still dozing, it was the driver who first spotted the six huge columns of the temples of Baalbek. He pointed out the columns to Mr. Akkawi, who turned excitedly to the boys seated behind him and called out, "As-Salamo to you Baalbek, the god of the Sun." These were the first words of a poem written by the poet laureate of Lebanon in honour of Baalbek, which my class had studied in our Arabic literature class. We were startled out of our dozing state by the teacher's voice, and on recognizing his words, we recited in unison the balance of the poem. There were several minutes of high excitement as the bus drew closer to the temple columns and the beautiful words of poetry echoed through the bus.

Soon thereafter the bus entered the streets of Baalbek where herds of sheep and goats shared the streets with dogs, camels, donkeys, carts and street vendors selling food items and other popular merchandise including all kinds of tourist souvenirs. The streets were packed and the bus driver was forced to inch his way slowly and patiently through the crowds. He was using his horn liberally to warn man and animal alike of the passage of his bus. It was almost 15 minutes after we first entered the city that the bus finally crossed over a small arched bridge linking the city to the temple grounds and pulled up to the main entrance. The excited boys were bouncing in the seats and the aisle, anxious to get close to the huge columns and run their hands over the smooth stones. The image of the temple was ingrained in our minds after years of seeing it on book covers, newspapers, packaging, billboards and currency bills.

Mr. Akkawi was first off the bus and had us gather in a group by the side of the bus while he went to speak to the admission officer and pay the entrance fees on behalf of the group. We stood quietly, gazing up in awe at the towering columns. The peaceful state did not last long, however, and we were soon talking and arguing about the shape of the columns that formed the different buildings in the temple. Once he had completed the financial transactions with the admissions officer, Mr. Akkawi waved us over to join him at the gate. He ushered the group through the gate and stood back to let us start running immediately towards the standing columns. An earthquake that had shaken the area centuries before had left shattered columns scattered in different areas and there were other structures to explore on the temple grounds, but Mr. Akkawi knew it was the standing columns that would first attract us. He watched as we ran our hands down the columns and marvelled at how smooth they felt and he chuckled to himself as he watched us hold hands and extend our arms around the base of one of the columns to see how many of us boys were needed to encircle it, just as every class before us had done. This year, it took five boys!

Soon, Mr. Akkawi stepped back into his role as teacher and began to point out to us the intricate sculpture at the top of the columns and the beams that joined them together. Identical pieces could be found where they had fallen to the ground and we gathered around the stonework to marvel at the beauty and intricacy of the work. The main feature was an egg and dart motif, which symbolized the continuity of life in the universe. The main temple had 54 columns before the earthquake toppled it. Giant pieces of the columns lay strewn about, some covered with debris, and other pieces had been carted away by marauding invaders who took pieces of the columns home to be erected as monuments to their victory. Remnants of smaller temples were also scattered around the main temple grounds and Mr. Akkawi explained that the smaller temples had been dedicated to the various gods worshipped by the local people in that time, for example, Jupiter the god of the people and ruler of all other gods, Bacchus, the god of wine and revelry, and Venus, the goddess of spring, beauty and love.

Eli and I were enthralled by what we saw and began imagining out loud what boys our age might have done in those days. What did they study, play and eat? Did they look the same as Eli and I? How were the temples built and the columns erected? Our fascination increased with each passing moment as we explored the relics on the temple grounds but we were finally riveted by the sculpture of the head of a lion, from whose roaring mouth water fell into a cistern in a courtyard near the temple of Bacchus. The lion's features were clearly carved and surprisingly, despite the wide-open mouth and sharp teeth, he appeared to be content with his role!

The class toured around the temple grounds for almost three hours before Mr. Akkawi judged it was time to head over to the market for drinks, snacks and souvenirs before getting back on the bus to return to Beirut. We filed out through the temple gate, more subdued than when we arrived, but quickly perking up at the sight of the numerous street vendors waiting for us with great patience. Falafel and halvah and other sweets were the snack of choice. Many also bought wood and leather knickknacks featuring various aspects of the temple. After ample time, Mr. Akkawi announced that we were to be back on the bus in 15 minutes as we had a long drive ahead of us to Beirut. When the time to leave rolled around, and Mr. Akkawi did a head count, he realized that Eli, Mohamed and I were missing. One of the students said he had last seen the three of us at one of the street stalls, trying on head-dresses. When Mr. Akkawi asked at the stall, the vendor said we had already left, after purchasing head-dresses, but he could not say which direction we had gone in. Mr. Akkawi worriedly began to pace through the stalls, looking for us. Finally, as he neared the end of the street of shops, he spotted three boys, wearing kafiyeh (head-dress) and agal (braided crown), sitting on the bank of the small river that flowed past the ruins. We appeared to be trying to feed the fish living in the murky water. Mr. Akkawi relieved, but with disbelief at our casualness echoing in his voice, hollered out our names and ordered us back to the bus immediately. We were startled out of our peaceful pastime, jumped up, but we slipped in the mud on the riverbank, sliding down and streaking our pants with wet mud. Mr. Akkawi herded us quickly back to the bus, lecturing and gesturing at us all the way on our irresponsibility. We were greeted with laughter and jeers from the other boys for being naughty, dirty and stupid. With all the students finally accounted for, the bus left Baalbek at 3:00 PM. Most of us boys were tired out from our day at the ruins and slept most of the way back to Beirut. When the bus arrived in Beirut at 6:30 PM, it was still light out and we were able to make it home before dark after being let out at our school.

I was happy to be home as my aunt Marie had promised the family a gourmet meal for our Sunday dinner, similar to the one Mrs. Andrawos prepared for her a week ago. Mrs. Andrawos was one of Aunt Marie's preferred customers. On Saturday, Marie and my grandmother went out to the European farmers' market to purchase the special vegetables for Sunday dinner. Early Sunday morning Marie was up before everybody else in the apartment and had already started preparations for dinner by the time the rest of the family appeared for breakfast. Mrs. Andrawos had written the recipe and instructions for Marie on her personal stationery, with her name embossed at the top in classic Roman script. Mrs. Andrawos was the matron of a very wealthy family that set the norms for all wealthy Lebanese families. Marie was deeply enamoured of her employer, treating her every idea and opinion with the greatest respect. Marie's excitement at preparing Mrs. Andrawos' special dinner was infectious and her mother and her sister Badre were soon drawn into the preparations. It took the three of them most of the morning and part of the afternoon to prepare the dinner and set the table and decorate it with beautiful flowers. When the family finally sat down, our expectations were high indeed. Marie carefully instructed us on the proper procedure and sequence of eating the special vegetable. We began first by sampling the artichokes a la Andrawos. The artichokes had been boiled so that the leaves could be peeled off in layers and sucked as an appetizer. The small matter in each leaf is hardly worth sucking, even though they have a tasty but tangy mellow flavour. The leaves were tasty but of small substance and the family eagerly waited for the main course, which turned out to consist of plain, boiled, buttered and especially-flavoured rice and artichoke hearts cooked with lamb cubes, onions, garlic, lemon and butter. Marie had also prepared the traditional Tabouleh salad dish and selected for dessert the Ashta fruit. The Tabouleh is made of a mixture of cracked boiled wheat, tomatoes, parsley, green onions, olive oil, lemon, and salt and all spice pepper mixture. It is a very tasty, nutritious, filling and delicious salad. The Ashta fruit is eaten in a fashion similar to eating the artichoke leaves and the substance is also small but creamy with a fruity sweet taste. By the time the meal was finished, the family had been sitting for almost two hours. Every one thanked Marie for her efforts; but shortly thereafter we heard uncle Sabih's stomach gurgle and he looked straight at Marie and asked her: "Where is the stuffing to fill my stomach?" Everyone laughed, even Marie, who quickly realized that this meal was not enough for hard-working people and hence went into the kitchen to find something to help fill her brother's empty stomach. She came back with a cold dish of Mjadra, dropped it in front of Sabih and exclaimed, "Here is your stuffing!" Mjadra is made of lentils, rice and onion wings fried in olive oil, cinnamon, allspice pepper, salt, water and olive oil. It is a nutritious, delicious and filling food that can be enjoyed either hot or cold.

The academic year flew by and before I knew it, we were in the final month, reviewing our subjects in preparation for the national government exams. Each school in Lebanon was asked to provide a set of questions to the Department of Education which would then set the questions for the exam, revising them as appropriate. The students would write the exams in government school buildings located in each district in Beirut. Three days were set aside for the exams and a registration number was assigned to each student. The results would be posted at each school about three weeks after the exams were finished, using the registration numbers as the sole identification. During the next three weeks, the students would resume their studies at their own schools and also write final exams set by their own school. When the results were posted, Eli,

Mohamed and I were all in the top 10 per cent in the country and I received the highest award in my class for our own school exams. It was an exciting and rewarding time for the three of us.

My young aunt, Badre, had also taken the national exams and passed with flying colours. Few girls in Lebanon continued their studies beyond the "elementary certificate", staying home to prepare for marriage or moving on to secretarial work to help their families financially. Badre planned to find secretarial work, contrary to her mother's wishes, and the entire family was soon drawn into the discussions and arguments about Badre's future. The subject of Badre's future came up one day while the parish priest was visiting and Badre's mother took advantage of the opportunity to ask the priest for his advice, secure in the knowledge that he would back up her opinion on the subject. The priest, weighing his words carefully, told Badre that he believed that the best place for women was in the home and quoted some passages from the Bible to support his belief. Badre responded that the world was changing and she did not want to live in the past. The priest, Father Jacob, then responded that the workplace was not conducive to proper morality even though he had full confidence in Badre's personal morals and ability to look after herself. He then went ahead to give the analogy of finding oneself in a crowd of people who start to sing and clap; sooner or later, as long as you are in the crowd, you will feel compelled to join the singing and the clapping. Badre, feeling cornered, decided to excuse herself from the room and went outside into the courtyard. I followed, feeling that she might need my support.

"You should do what you want, despite what Father Jacob has said," I told Badre.

Badre and I talked together for a while then went back into the apartment where the priest, Badre's mother and other members of the family were still visiting. Badre stated to everyone present that she was sure of the correctness of her decision and that working as a secretary was all she wanted to do. Nabiha, Badre's mother, turned to Father Jacob for further support, but he simply smiled and said that when he wanted to join the priesthood, his parents had tried to dissuade him, but he prayed very hard for God's help and, eventually, his parents relented. Father Jacob smiled and looked at Badre and suggested she should do the same. With that, the priest took his leave. Sitto Nabiha, with tears in her eyes, reached out and hugged Badre and wished her the best in following her own dreams.

General view of Shweir, 1994

My birthplace in Shweir, 1994

My parents Wadih and Ward, 1973

Jiddo Fadlallah, 1952

Sitto Nabiha, 1950

Aunt Marie, 1968

Aunt Badre, 1968

Uncle Sabih, 1968

My great aunts Nabiha and Haifa Simon of Jackson, Mississippi, 1967

Jiddo Fadlallah and his general store, Miami, Arizona, 1925

Jiddo Fadlallah's home and general store, Miami, Arizona, 2004

My father and Uncle Gibran, 1968

Cousin Elias and his son Nasr, 1968

Shweir Flayceh slopes, 1994

Ain El Tahtah, abandoned Shweir water well, 1994; Abandoned Shweir main street, 1994

View of Beirut from the mountain. *Photo by Telko Sport, 1950*

View of Beirut and Sunnine mountain. *Photo by Telko Sport, 1950*

Elementary school in Beirut, 1994

Elementary school in Shweir, 1994

Sidon Castle and fishermen's net, 1994

Sidon abandoned old city street, 1994

Baalbek standing columns, 1994

Egg and dart sculpture in Baalbek, 1994

Cleopatra's sculpture in Baalbek, 1994

My son John trying to tip over one of the Baalbek columns, 1994

Lion's sculptured head in Baalbek, 1994

Cedar Arz tree in Lebanon, 1994

The Nuns school in Shweir, 1994

The Nuns school playground and Oak tree in Shweir, 1994

Nahr Abu Dawood river, 1994

Abu Dawood's grandson Anwar and me on the way to Miami, Arizona, 2004.
Photo by A.G. Kenicer, 2004

International College, 1994

Kitchen at International College, 1994

American University of Beirut. *Photo by John Waterbury, AUB president, 2004*

My son John and me, West Hall, AUB campus, 1994

New residential area in Ramleh Baida white sand district, Beirut. *Photo by Telko Sport, 1984*

The famous rock Rawsheh Pigeon Grotto, Beirut. *Photo by Telko Sport, 1984*

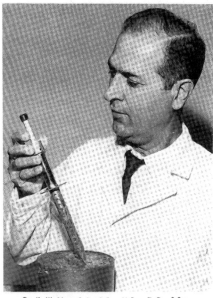

Dr. K. W. Nasser B.A., B.Sc., M.Sc., Ph.D., P.Eng.,
M.E.I.C., M.A.C.I., F.A.S.C.E.
Professor of Civil Engineering, University of Saskatchewan

How the 'K' Slump Tester was born!

"It was during one of my concrete lectures that I wondered aloud as to why should we be satisfied by the awkward 'slump' test which has not been improved since it was first introduced in 1913," said Professor Nasser[1]. "That thought kept bugging me on many occasions and so I decided to try and do something about it."

"I started by searching all the relevant publications and found out that several instruments were proposed and used, but none was simple enough to dislodge the slump test even though some were based on rigorous scientific principles. After a few meditations, I came up with a contraption that can be described as rich in principles, but poor in practicality and now it serves as a paper weight on one of the shelves in my office."

A few other ideas and trials followed, but some of them ended as decorations in collectors' basements. Finally, on one of those long, dark December nights the probe was conceived and brought to light shortly thereafter. It is basically a calibrated, hollow tube about 12 inches long and 3/4 inches in diameter which can be inserted into fresh concrete by hand. It has a solid, conical end for easy insertion, a round disc that controls the depth of penetration, and two groups of openings through which the wet concrete can enter the tube. The level of concrete in the probe, indicated on the plunger scale, denotes the 'slump' quality of the concrete.

The probe is simple and economical to use and reduces testing time. Also it is the first device which can measure the consolidation of concrete after it is placed in the forms. It has the added advantage that it does not need a highly trained engineer or technologist to operate it.

Another asset is that no calibration is required. A simple field comparison check against a 'slump' test will prove its accuracy.

[1] Ref. Saskatchewan Engineer 1972

The 3 pictures above show how versatile the 'K' tester is on the site.

The K-Slump and Flow Tester, 1973

KARIM NASSER PREPARES WHEAT DISH —Star-Phoenix Photo

Tasty wheatkey concocted by engineer turned cook

Take some wheat and grind it up. Take some lean beef and grind that too. Throw in a dash of seasoning — Presto —a wheatkey.

Although the name is new, the ingredients aren't. Anyone who has been to Lebanon will recognize the dish.

Karim Nasser says he thinks he can help in his own small way to promote wheat sales — and he's put up some money to prove it.

Mr. Nasser, a native of Lebanon but a Canadian for the past 10 years, is a professor of engineering at the university.

He makes no attempt to disguise the fact that what he knows about wheat wouldn't occupy more than a couple of minutes of discussion.

But he does know that in his native country, the wheatkey is as common to his people as roast beef is to Canadians.

"The seasonings are a bit different," Mr. Nasser says in describing his made-in-Canada product, but it's still the same two basic ingredients.

In Lebanon it is the main plate of many meals.

Mr. Nasser says he can't foresee any difficulties that would prevent it from being equally as well received here in Canada.

The wheatkey might be mistaken for a hamburger, for it is shaped like one. Even the prices are relatively the same, from 40 to 90 cents for the wheatkey deluxe.

The wheatkey can even be baked, broiled, grilled or fried.

But talking about a product isn't enough. So Mr. Nasser diversified and is now the owner of a cafe.

"I bought the cafe mainly to promote the wheatkey," Mr. Nasser says.

"If its a success I'll make a few dollars — if its a failure I'll lose a few."

Flipping Wheatkey Burger, *Saskatoon StarPhoenix*, 1974

Cement tester used in Toronto

A Saskatchewan designed and built cement tester is being used to help build the tallest self-supporting structure in the world.

The instrument, called the K slump tester, is being used to test concrete in the CN communications tower in Toronto, as it is constructed to its 1,800-foot height.

The tester, invented by Prof. K. W. Nasser of the department of engineering, University of Saskatchewan, Saskatoon, and built by Smith-Roles Ltd. of Saskatoon, is being used where traditional machines prove to be awkward.

The invention tests the "runniness" of concrete after it has been poured into forms. The old method of testing required a large amount of cement to be poured into a cone slump tester and then packed until solid.

Construction Testing Services Ltd., of Rexdale, Ontario is using the tester and an official of the company wrote to Prof. Nasser that his invention can be used where the old method would be impractical.

The tower takes shape as the molding form slides upwards.

The K-Slump used in the CN Tower, Toronto, *Saskatoon StarPhoenix,* **1974**

A danger of chauvinism

Of particular interest to a university town like Saskatoon are the latest figures on the national origins of teachers working on Canadian campuses. There are widely differing attitudes toward the importance of this nationality question in the education of our students.

Statistics Canada reports for the 1971-72 academic year about 63.3 per cent "Canadian content" among full-time teachers in the universities of this country: a small increase of 2.4 per cent over the previous year.

The United States contributed15.4 per cent of all faculty members in Canada, and the rest of them 21.3 per cent came from Britain, France and other countries.

There are those who are gravely concerned over the presence of foreign born and foreign educated instructors in our schools and colleges. One aggressive group of academics is pushing hard for a minimum Canadian faculty content of 85 per cent.

There is virtue in this if the Canadians hired are as well qualified as those who are brought from abroad. There is danger in it if the mere fact of Canadianism cuts off the employment of those who may be more highly qualified than our own scholars.

The largest percentage of U.S. professors on our campuses are those teaching the fine and applied arts, 28.8 per cent of the totals in these fields of study. It could very well be argued such instructors may tend to discolour a purely Canadian culture through the addition to it of valuable outside influences; that fewer than 30 per cent of our fine arts professors cannot dominate the other 70 per cent ; and, indeed, that this much imported creativity saves Canadian culture from becoming inbred.

The fault, if there is a fault, does not lie entirely with our university administrators. For example, one local university department head reports he offered the chance of a good position to two well-qualified Canadian applicants; and each of them in turn reneged on his application because he preferred to take up an offer from a U.S. college.

In such departments, as Canadian history, political science, or teacher training, there is good reason to favor Canadians over even more highly qualified foreigners. But this is not so in subjects of less strictly nationalistic importance. Any university would be silly to turn down Albert Einstein just because a Canadian Ph. D. happened also to be available. This may explain why the number of British professors teaching in Canada is highest, 13.1 per cent in the areas of physics and mathematics.

However, there really is an ever-modest tendency among us to favor foreigners, just because they come from distant places; and Canadians must try to overcome this sense of our own inferiority. Too many of us subscribe to Saint Mathews dictum: "A prophet is not without honor, save in his own country and his own house."

At the same time, we must guard against the kind of chauvinism which would raise barriers against an international free-trade in brains and competence.

Congratulations due

K.W. Nasser, professor of civil engineering on the university's Saskatoon campus, is to be congratulated not only for his inventive contribution to the construction industry, but also for the manner in which he has applied his discovery to the economic well-being of this community.

Prof. Nasser invented the K-slump tester, a device which measures the workability and compaction of fresh concrete. Orders for this quality-control tool have been received from concrete suppliers, commercial testers, government departments and others all the way from British Columbia to Newfoundland and from the United States. It is being patented in Canada, U.S., the United Kingdom, Germany, Australia and Japan.

Since unveiling his invention last year at a convention in Buffalo, New York, Prof. Nasser has received many attractive offers to have this new device manufactured in the U.S. He has decided, however, to have it produced where it was invented, right here in Saskatoon, where it is now being manufactured by a local engineering firm.

"We are part of this community," says Prof. Nasser, "and when the opportunity arises to create employment here, we should seize it."

It should be of some interest to those ultra-nationalistic academics, who are trying to discourage the employment of foreign-born faculty members, that Prof. Nasser was born and educated in Lebanon. What price "Canadian content" on our campuses when we can profit so much from the brilliance and the good citizenship of such "foreigners" as this?

A danger of chauvinism, Editor, *Saskatoon StarPhoenix,* **1973**

Man with a vision

☐ Victory
Construction
founder's foresight
has served him well
in real estate,
business
and academia

The **Exec.** file

By Murray Lyons

Karim (Kay) Nasser hasn't been afraid to try new things in business even if he was, as his family puts it, a little ahead of his time.

The founder of the Saskatoon real estate investment company Victory Construction Ltd. has, at various times, operated a restaurant and a grocery store to ensure commercial space in his properties didn't go empty.

His daughter Mona says the type of healthy, Middle East food offered by her father's restaurant would likely find its audience in today's Saskatoon.

"He was about 20 years ahead of his time with that one," says Mona, a lawyer by training, who is now president and chief executive officer of Victory Majors Investment Co.

It's the new publicly traded company that will be buying the real estate portfolio of 30 buildings, including 300 apartment suites, her father built up over the years.

Nasser was also likely ahead of his time in some aspects of commercial real estate. During the past 10 years his company bought up a number of properties in downtown Saskatoon at a time when undervalued downtown property was severely taxed under the old assessment rules.

One building Victory purchased, the former London Building on 20th Street, had actually been abandoned for nearly 20 years. After several years of paying taxes with no rent coming in, Nasser and his colleagues made the decision to convert the upper three floors to apartments.

The building, now renamed The Vienna, was fully rented before it was even completed. Nasser is optimistic the main floor, kept for commercial purposes, will be rented soon.

The company also owns a number of properties along Second Avenue. "Some people left the downtown, but I still feel the downtown is a very important part of the city."

Nasser's loyalty to Saskatoon is strong even though, when he came here more than 35 years ago, it was with the intention of getting his doctorate in civil engineering at the University of Saskatchewan under Neville Adams and then moving on.

Nasser had already one degree in engineering from the American University in Beirut and his master's from Kansas, which he had obtained while working for the Trans Arabian Pipeline company.

Returning to Lebanon to get married, he then ended up in North Bay, Ont. where he managed a concrete company — no real surprise since the study of concrete had become his life's work in academia.

Construction was also in the family's blood as his father owned a construction company in Lebanon, working in both concrete and stone.

By the time he arrived in Saskatoon to finish his doctorate, the Nassers already had three children. Just as he finished up his doctorate, Prof. Adams moved to Calgary and the U of S appointed Nasser for a one-year term.

"I didn't want to stay more than even one year," Nasser recalls. "One year went into a second year and a third year ..."

Nasser just retired recently after 30 years as a tenured professor in Saskatoon. But teaching was only part of his engineering life.

"In all engineering colleges, they encourage professors to do work outside and I didn't need too much encouragement because of my background," Nasser said. "I was just basically growing up doing work in construction."

Early on in Saskatoon, he decided to build an apartment block.

"I had almost nothing. I went to the bank, talked to the manager there. He looked into my background. . . . My credit to start was $5,000. I didn't have any downpayment.

"But they loaned me money to start a small apartment building."

Man with a Vision, Murray Lyons, Saskatoon StarPhoenix, 1999

The result was an eight-suite unit in the 2400-block of Seventh Street East.

It's still in the Victory Companies portfolio as is almost every other apartment and commercial building the company has built or purchased over the years.

The pattern established in that summer of 1964 continued with more apartment buildings going up in subsequent summers under Nasser's supervision.

"It was one or two a summer, whatever I could handle," he recalls. "As long as you're paying the mortgage, you have no difficulties."

It wasn't always easy to do that. A few years after starting, there was a downturn in the city's economy and suites were going empty.

Nasser moved his family, now with five children, into two of the suites for a period of time just so someone was paying the mortgage.

Victory Construction survived that as well as the period of sky-high mortgages in the early 1980s. It diversified out of apartments through buying small commercial properties; the Avalon shopping plaza was the first.

U of S commerce professor John Brennan says it's no surprise to him an engineering professor would show such entrepreneurial instincts.

"I think you will find among the engineering faculty a pretty strong entrepreneurial spirit," Brennan said, noting the example of Ben Torchinsky, who started the now-huge Canadian contracting company Agra, when he was on the U of S engineering faculty.

Brennan first worked with Nasser in the Canadian Club.

"He's the guy who came and twisted my arm and got me to join the executive," Brennan remembers. "I wasn't conscious of the size nor the success of the real estate portfolio."

Among his other community work, Nasser was an adviser to the Saskatoon Convalescent Home and president of the organization when a new building was constructed.

Having arrived in Canada when John Diefenbaker was prime minister, Nasser even caught the political bug for one provincial election, running unsuccessfully for the PCs during the years when Dick Collver was trying to revive the party.

In his professional life, several of his inventions related to the concrete industry were accepted by the American Society of Testing and Materials, most noteworthy being the Kay-Slump tester which tests the slumping ability of concrete, an important test of how well it has been mixed.

It was first used when the CN Tower was being constructed but Nasser decided royalties on these inventions should go to the university.

Brennan recently joined the board of directors of the new Victory Majors Investments company formed last month when the Nasser family began turning their real estate portfolio over into a new junior capital company listed on the Alberta Stock Exchange.

"There was never any question in my

mind about the strength of Kay Nasser and family," Brennan said. "They are solid, highly ethical, exactly the kinds of people I like to be involved with in public companies."

Nasser says one of the reasons his real estate portfolio is being turned over into the new public company is so his five children can know the value of the shares of the company, including children who pursued law and medicine and aren't interested in the business.

"Some of them are not interested in the business. That way they can go their own way and they know what their shares are worth," he said.

Besides daughter Mona, Kay's son John, a recent U of S MBA graduate is involved with Victory's management as is nephew Gaby Akl, who came to Saskatoon from Beirut a number of years ago and became portfolio manager.

Despite his success as a developer and owner of real estate, Nasser says he still considers himself a university professor at heart.

"I enjoyed teaching very much and doing research has always been part of me. Even now I still go to the university and do whatever I can. Teaching seems to be my calling more than construction."

— SP Photo by Richard Marjan

Karim Nasser recently retired after 30 years of teaching at the U of S

The Good Neighbour by Beverly Fast

"I am part of all that I have met." The words belong to Alfred, Lord Tennyson. The thinking behind them is shared by many, including Dr. Karim (Kay) Nasser, PhD'65.

For almost 40 years, Dr. Nasser and his family have been quietly donating to the U of S. What began as a $200 annual donation is today a $200,000 family endowment that funds 10 scholarships to U of S students every year.

Such growth seems to surprise even Dr. Nasser, now Professor Emeritus in the College of Engineering. He shrugs modestly, though there's a smile in his eyes. He knows he's making a real difference in students' lives.

Dr. Nasser is one of many alumni donors whose modest but consistent gifts have made remarkable things possible. He practices a quiet philanthropy and only agreed to the interview with the *Green & White* because he believes it might provide an example to others. "There may be people who want to support the University, but can't see a way to do it. And there is a way, there are many ways," he says.

After earning his PhD in 1965, Dr. Nasser joined the College of Engineering. He made his first donation in 1967. He continued to give something every year thereafter. As his teaching career flourished, his research also began paying dividends in the form of marketable inventions. The first, the K-Slump Tester, was introduced to the world during the construction of the CN Tower. Dr. Nasser donated royalties earned from the invention to the U of S.

"It was a family decision, based on loyalty to the community," Dr. Nasser says. "I was raised with the idea that you are good to your neighbours, and the U of S is more than my good neighbour.

"I also feel that as human beings, we should try to do the best we can for future generations. If I hadn't had help when I was starting university, I wouldn't have made it. I wanted to give something back that would benefit students, like myself, who were anxious to get an education but also had financial need."

Life has rewarded Dr. Nasser and his family, and he continues to expand his gifts to the U of S. He recently committed $50,000 to fund two new scholarships in the College of Engineering.

He has also made a bequest of land, a quarter section located across the road from the College of Agriculture's research station. Purchased in the 1980s, the land has grown significantly in value. In recent years the Nasser family has leased it to the University for a nominal stipend. The land is being used to grow test crops under development at the U of S – with exciting results.

Research is close to Dr. Nasser's heart, and this success inspired him to gift the land to the University in his will.

As colleague, teacher, mentor, friend and benefactor, Dr. Kay Nasser is indeed a part of all that he has met… and will continue to be long into the future. ∎

The Good Neighbour, Beverly Fast, *Green & White*, University of Saskatchewan Alumni Magazine, 2005

4 Summer in Shweir, Declaration of World War II and Back to Shweir Elementary School

O nce the elementary school year in Beirut was over, many of the students and I returned to our villages. I was excited to return home to Shweir and looked forward to telling my parents that I had passed the national exams and won the award for the highest marks in my class. I had even received a prize, a book of poems written by Mr. Mikhail, my teacher. My parents were very pleased to hear about my good performance at school, but unsure what it would mean for my future. They wondered whether to have me continue with my studies or to have me leave school to learn a trade, either to be a stone mason, like my father, a truck driver, like Jerjy, a next-door relative and neighbour, or to pick up another trade. They did not discuss their thoughts with me, choosing instead to wait until Sabih came to visit and to seek his advice in the matter. I was oblivious to the debate, which would affect my future and was simply basking in my holiday time. I seemed to have unlimited free time, with the exception of the odd chores around the garden or house, such as watering the vegetables, picking up groceries or delivering lunch to my father at his work site.

I was the centre of attention for the first few days after I returned to Shweir as my friends, Elias, Wadih, Najm, Chafic, Najib, Bahij, Edmond and Sami wanted to hear about my adventures in the big city. As none of the group of my friends had work other than minor family chores, we quickly re-established our routines from the summer before I had left for Beirut. One day, we decided to head to the Amineh's orchard to pick green pine cones for a snack. As we neared the orchard, Elias noticed Mrs. Amineh working among the trees, and cautioned the group to continue innocently past the orchard, pausing only to greet Mrs. Amineh in the nicest manner possible. We felt certain that our naughty intentions were well-hidden, but our confidence was shattered when Mrs. Amineh stated that whenever we were ready to return home, she would like us to help her carry a load of dried pine leaves that she was collecting for her bread baking. Without saying so directly, Mrs. Amineh had shown that she knew perfectly well why the gang was sauntering past her orchard. We boys sauntered on, looking for another spot to carry out our raid away from Mrs. Amineh. Eventually, we reached a secluded area where we found some good pine trees and a spring surrounded by lush shrubs. The spring flowed into a small slough, which held a few colonies of loudly chirping frogs. We quickly swarmed up the pine trees to pick the best cones, bringing our treasure back to the ground where we eagerly and quickly ate the fruit, this being the first crop of the year. We traded stories about our recent adventures, told jokes and horsed around. I suggested we all jump into the slough for a swim, but my suggestion was rejected, as none of my friends knew how to swim. There were no swimming pools in our village and we were far from the sea. None of the boys had ever learned how to swim. With great pride and confidence in my voice, I informed my friends that I would teach them how to swim as I had learned in Beirut. The gang hesitated, so to encourage them I stripped off my clothes and jumped into the cool spring water, flailing my hands and kicking my feet to impress my friends with my skill. It worked, and one by one, the group agreed to join me. The water was only waist deep, so the six friends, once all of them had taken off their clothes and jumped in, started fooling around and splashing each other, imitating my actions.

When we were tired, we crawled out together and lay in the sun, waiting for the sun to warm us up. Najm, Najib and Edmond, who were older and more developed than the others, curled their pubic hair to look like moustaches and told us to look at Nassib's moustache, Nassib being the village Natour or patrolman. We all roared with laughter, and those who could, tried to imitate Najm and Edmond. Suddenly, Nassib appeared from behind a bush. We boys scrambled to grab our clothes and cover ourselves, but the patrolman was faster. He scooped our clothes into one big pile and sat on them and began to lecture us about stealing pine cones. By threatening to tell our parents about our escapade and promising to haul each one into the municipal office for a beating if he caught us again, he was able to extract a promise from us that we would not return to the orchards again, nor would we steal any other fruit, whatever the season. Once the promises were given, the Natour returned our clothes and once dressed, we turned and ran off at high speed.

Several days later, three of my friends and I went hunting for small birds in the vineyards and fig groves. Our guns were the kind where we needed to pack the powder and the pellets by hand. Legally, we needed a license to hunt with a firearm but hardly anyone in the village bothered with this technicality. We quickly found a grove full of singing birds and we spread ourselves throughout the trees, each hoping to hit at least one bird. Soon, shots could be heard from all directions and smoke streaked into the sky. The birds departed en masse, leaving nothing behind except a few ruffled feathers. My friends and I had regrouped to reload our guns when the village patrolman appeared from behind a bush and shouted at us to stay put. Instead, we ran in all directions as fast as our legs would carry us. The Natour concentrated on following and catching me, which he managed after a five-minute chase through the grove and nearby forest. The Natour grabbed at my gun, but I would not let go and we two were caught in a tug of war. The other boys, meanwhile, dropped off their guns at Salim's house and asked him to hide them. They then returned to the grove to see how I was faring in my struggle with the patrolman and to plead with him to let me go. The Natour told them he was going to arrest every single one of them instead, which caused the boys to start yelling at him. He was still in a standoff with me, the gun going back and forth between us, when Salim and his father, Boutros, soon joined the group. Boutros tried to intercede, to no avail. When his words fell on deaf ears, Boutros, who was a large, well-muscled man, decided to get physical and reached in to jerk the gun away from both Nassib and me. He then shouted at the Natour, in a loud and firm voice, to let the boys go or he would use his muscles on him. Salim, the other boys and I saw our opportunity and quickly turned tail and ran away, leaving the Natour behind shouting back at Boutros about the law. The last thing I heard as I quickly looked back over my shoulder was Boutros admonishing the Natour to be lenient with the boys and tell their parents about their actions instead of threatening them and taking away their guns.

We all gathered at Salim's house and waited for Boutros to come home. When he finally arrived, we excitedly thanked him, but Boutros calmed us down and gave us a stern lecture about the careful handling of guns. We were quick to agree with whatever Boutros said as he was well-known as one of the strong men of the village and people were careful not to antagonize him. Meanwhile, the Natour vented his anger by threatening each of us as we finally headed home, promising he would have help the next time he tried to catch us.

The next escapade started when my friend, Fouad Touma, and I decided to go swimming in Abu Dawood's river. None of the other boys would join us as they were worried about the Natour's threats and swimming in Abu Dawood's river was not permitted. It was a still, hot, sunny day as Fouad and I followed the trails through the forest to the river. Swarms of butterflies fluttered from flower to flower, the cicadas were singing in the bushes and trees and the birds were jumping among the branches of the fig trees, enjoying the ripe figs and teasing Fouad and me who could not shoot at them that day. Occasionally, either Fouad or I would pick up a stone and hurl it at one of the birds, but our efforts were met with indifference and more teasing. After a half-hour stroll through the forest, Fouad and I reached the river, which ran through a sharp fold between two hills. The riverbanks were thickly covered with shrubs and trees. It was a narrow river, small by any standards, which could be easily crossed by tiptoeing over the rocks which protruded from the water. However, at one point Abu Dawood had built a stone wall to dam the water and create a small reservoir, which he used to irrigate his garden. Usually, the water was about seven feet deep, but today it sat around the four-foot mark as Abu Dawood had just watered his garden that morning. We stripped off our clothes, tucked them under one of the nearby bushes and cautiously approached the edge of the water. I slipped into the reservoir first and began to flail my arms and kick with my legs, but despite my efforts I did not float very well. Fouad was scared and refused to jump in until I pointed out a ladder lying near the edge of the reservoir. Fouad picked up the ladder and laid it on the surface of the water where it floated by itself. I told Fouad that he could hang on to the ladder if he had trouble floating. This was enough to encourage Fouad to jump in. Once in the water Fouad tried to imitate my style of floating and swimming but he could not keep his head above water. Feeling a little worried, he grabbed at the ladder to hang on and float, but the ladder sank with his weight. At this, Fouad became frantic, pulling harder at the ladder and causing it to sink more. I tried to help Fouad by grabbing the ladder to steady it, but again, with the extra weight, the ladder sank below the surface of the water. Both of us started to panic and were grabbing frantically at the sinking ladder when suddenly one end of the ladder hit the bottom of the reservoir and stuck in the mud, leaving the other end sticking out above the water's surface. Fouad, who was a little taller than me, realized that his toes would also reach the mud at the bottom of the reservoir, allowing him to stand up and keep his head and shoulders out of the water. He calmed down and reached to me, as I was still pounding and flailing the water, and tapped me on the shoulder and told me to take it easy and simply stand up. I allowed my legs to sink until my feet hit bottom and slowly stood up and relaxed my arms. After a few minutes of calm and silence, both of us began to laugh and cry at the same time. Finally, we crawled out of the reservoir, dried ourselves and made our way home, with heavy hearts and prayers of thanks to God and St. Peter, for saving our lives.

One week later, my uncle Gibran told me that he was taking his four cows to a neighbouring village to marry them to the Fahl, the bull with the best reputation in the district. Uncle Gibran said I could go with him and bring a couple of my friends, too, if I wanted. This sounded exciting to me, as I had never before heard of cattle getting married. I ran out to invite Wadih, Elias and Chafic, who in turn got excited at the idea and asked their parents for permission to go. With permission granted, we four boys turned up the next morning on Uncle Gibran's doorstep, ready to join him for the trip to the next village. Uncle Gibran had anticipated that we would show up early and had lined up some chores for us to do before we could leave on our road trip. By 8:30, the chores were done and Gibran directed each one of us to take one cow by her chain and lead them behind him and his dog, Dabool, a fat but clever sheep dog. Gibran was a chain smoker in his 60s, but he was in excellent health and trotted off at a quick pace, we four trailing behind him, leading the cows. We walked in a single file through the narrow, cobbled streets of the town until we came to a wide country trail skirting a meadow. Here, Gibran told us to let the cows loose to graze before we continued on our journey. The four boys then sprawled around Uncle Gibran and listened intently as he explained how virile Fahl was and how most of the cows from the neighbouring villages would go to Fahl to get married. Elias asked how and why cows got married, as he had never heard of such a thing before. Gibran explained that Fahl had a penis, which would become erect and then be inserted into the vagina of the cow. Semen would be ejected from the penis into the vagina to fertilize the eggs in the cow and the cow would then become pregnant. After a while, the cow would give birth to baby cows. Gibran carried on to tell us that all animals, even cats and dogs, and interestingly enough, even humans, get married in a similar fashion in order to conceive and have babies. Uncle Gibran's frankness and candid explanation of the mystery of pregnancy and the birth of babies was fascinating to us boys. Nobody had ever told us anything about having babies in this fashion before. This was our first lesson about sex, marriage and procreation and it made a lasting impression.

We soon resumed our trip to the village where Fahl's owner was ready and waiting for the cows. Gibran and Fahl's owner discussed the procedure together while the four boys hung over the fence and gaped at Fahl. It was decided to let one cow into the field at a time, initially keeping Fahl and the cow separated by a fence to allow them time to sniff each other out and get ready. At the appropriate time, Fahl's owner would open the gate that separated the two animals and we all watched as Fahl mounted the cow. Once all four cows had been impregnated, Gibran and the boys were invited in for a lunch of shish kebab, salad, laban and Arak for the men, to celebrate the successful mating of the animals. Gibran and Fahl's owner raised their glasses to toast each other's animals and wished each other's animals continued fertility and many successful matings. After lunch, the group headed home, Wadih, Elias, Chafic and I mulling over what we had seen and preparing the story we would tell the rest of our friends.

That summer, my father, Wadih, was working in Houran, Syria. It therefore fell on my shoulders to do more family chores than was normal for a boy my age. Rumours that Germany would start a war in Europe had raised fears in Shweir and throughout Lebanon and people were stockpiling provisions to tide them over the next few months or to the next season. Wheat, in particular, was in demand and when my mother and I heard that Rashid would be bringing in a truckload of wheat from Syria we went together to his home to place an order. For our order of 200 Kilos (two bags of 100 Kilos each), Rashid wanted LL20.00 in cash but my mother could only give him a down payment of LL5.00, explaining to Rashid that we were waiting for some money to come by mail from Abu Karim in Houran, Syria. This was fine, said Rashid, he could wait, but he wanted a promissory note for the balance, with 20 per cent interest. This was the first time I had heard of a promissory note and interest and it helped me realize the importance of cash to purchase goods or services.

It was a few days later that I noticed my mother and several of our neighbours hurriedly walking to the town doctor's house in order to hear the radio news. When I asked what news was going to be so interesting, my mother answered that the 5:00 PM London newscast was providing the most up-to-date news about the war. This was the first time I began to understand that there were serious events occurring outside of Shweir, which could affect the daily routines of my life. I decided to follow my mother to Dr.

Milhem's home, a few minutes away, where we found a large crowd assembled on the road and spilling into the square near the house. The doctor had placed the radio on his second floor balcony and raised the volume to its maximum. At 5:00 PM sharp, the famous chimes of Big Ben rang out over the airwaves and a surge of excitement rippled through the assembled crowd.

"In a summary of today's news, tension eases as the parties agree to continue negotiations," they heard the radio announcer say. The gathered neighbours slowly dispersed, quietly repeating to each other stories of famine and sickness from the previous world war. The same scene was repeated nightly for 12 days, but on the 13th day, when the neighbours gathered at Dr. Milhem's home once again for the nightly news summary, the news was different. Germany had invaded Poland and the allies, England and France, had declared war on Germany. The news sent shock waves through the gathered crowd, with the adults and the elderly hit especially hard for they remembered the suffering of the First World War. That evening, the crowd dispersed quickly in silence, children following their parents home, all absorbed in their own thoughts. At the Nasser home, everybody went to bed unnaturally early, as if the phantom of war would disappear with our dreams.

Early the next morning, Rashid came and pounded on our door to announce that the bags of wheat we had ordered had arrived from the Beka' valley. Luckily, my father had sent my mother some money just a few days earlier so she was ready and anxious to pick up the two bags of wheat. At Rashid's residence, my mother and I found many of our neighbours picking up their own purchases. My mother handed the money to Rashid, who took it, but appeared fidgety and did not speak for a long moment. Then he sighed and told my mother that the price of the wheat had doubled since war was declared and each bag would now cost LL20.00. This news staggered my mother and me. We had little money to spare. Both of us began to argue with Rashid, stating we had made the deal in good faith and had provided a down payment and promissory note with interest. How could he change his mind so suddenly? Rashid swore by Allah and all the saints that the suppliers had raised the prices and he was forced to do the same or lose money. My mother and I kept arguing that we had a legal agreement and he could not charge us a penny more! Besides, we could not and would not accept to pay any extra charge. The heated arguments continued for 10 minutes but Rashid would continue to fidget without budging. I got really very angry and impatient and started shouting insults at Rashid, wanting to hit him on the head, but our neighbour Michel interceded and helped settle the matter and forced Rashid to live with the terms of the agreement. Cursing Rashid and the war, my mother and I swore never to do business with him again.

My uncle Gibran had lent us his donkey and our neighbour Michel helped me load the bags of wheat onto the borrowed donkey. As we made our way home, leading the donkey, I told my mother how hurt and disappointed I was about having to deal with a dishonest person like Rashid. I had learned at home and at school that honesty was the best policy and I could not believe that my first exposure to business could be contrary to what I had learned. My mother calmed me down and took pains to assure me that not all businesspeople were like Rashid. There were many more that were kind, honest and decent. However, she could not hide her own disappointment and I noticed that my mother's brow was furrowed with worry. When I asked what was wrong, she explained she was thinking about how we would be able to buy wheat and other necessities once the family had consumed what we already had. We walked the rest of the way home in silence, each one lost in our own thoughts.

Once home, we were met by my younger sisters, who were excited about the donkey and wanted to go for a ride. I promised them they could do that after they helped me unload the wheat. It did not take long to transfer the wheat from the bags on the donkey's back to a large drum inside the house, using small pails to carry the wheat. Once the donkey had been unloaded, I helped my three sisters ride the donkey around the block as their reward, and then slowly walked the donkey back to my uncle's home. I told Uncle Gibran the whole story of the price gouging and he solemnly advised me never to deal with Rashid or his like again.

My summer holiday came to an abrupt end with the declaration of war. The serious and worried demeanour of my parents and the neighbours quickly affected the free spirits and happy mood of the children in the neighbourhood. Then, two days later the church bells began to ring early in the morning announcing a death in the village, adding more weight to the already solemn atmosphere in the village. Those who heard the bells rushed to their front doors, some still in their night-gowns, to inquire of their neighbours who had died. It was a great shock to my mother to see Edmond Touma sobbing and to hear that his brother Fouad, one of my best friends and one of my constant playmates, had died suddenly. Fouad was only 12 years old and had been playing with the rest of the gang just two days ago. The cause of his death was said to be sunstroke, which greatly saddened and puzzled me, and I wondered why Fouad would die from sunstroke when all of his friends had been playing together under the same sun! The news was devastating. His teacher came around to each home to ask Fouad's friends to participate in the funeral procession and to walk in pairs ahead of the casket. The funeral was a profoundly sad event for the whole town and the wailing and sobbing of the village women was overwhelming. As the funeral procession wound its way through the village, the sound of clucking chickens and barking dogs, mixed with the sound of tears, were forever imprinted in my memory. Fouad's death was particularly hard on me, as both of us had spent the whole summer together, the closest of friends. I tried to console myself by repeating many times the priest's affirmation that Fouad was in heaven and happy to be with Jesus.

Soon, it was time to be thinking of school again. As my father was still working in Syria, my mother spoke to my uncle Gibran and they decided I should stay in Shweir and go to the village school because of the difficulties caused by the war. I had mixed feelings about the decision. I was pleased to be going to school with my village friends but I knew I was going to miss the friends and teachers I had in Beirut.

The village school was run by the village priest with the help of two teachers hired from neighbouring towns. There were a few local teachers available, who chose not to apply for the positions, as the wages were very low. The school building was part of a nunnery, which had space for two elementary schools, one for boys and one for girls. Each school had two rooms on each side of the chapel and a small yard where the children could play during their breaks. There was no direct connection between the two schoolyards and the classrooms. The girls' yard had a massive oak tree standing in one corner while the boys' yard had only a mulberry tree. Each school had one bathroom, which was really an outhouse, and neither had running water. Drinking water was available from large pottery jars with drinking cups hanging from the jar handles. Also, the children could fetch a drink from the main village well Ain El Tahtah, which was only a stone's throw away from the school building. The school furniture was made of solid wood and consisted of tables and benches connected together, each one seating eight pupils in a row. The teacher in each room had a small podium, a table, a chair and a blackboard. Each room had a wood stove used for heat in the winter. It was the responsibility of each pupil to bring one piece of firewood to school each morning to help keep the building warm. When school opened during the first week in October, the students were divided into two groups, according to age. A teacher named Halim would teach the elementary students and Paul would teach the high school students. Both Halim and Paul were from Beirut, in their early twenties and had both just recently received their teaching certificates. Halim had dark skin and brown eyes, while Paul had light skin and blue eyes. The priest, Father Hatoum, gathered all students for an assembly where he welcomed them to the school, outlined the main rules and regulations that would govern their behaviour and then introduced Halim and Paul, who were warmly welcomed by the students. The students were then sent off to their classrooms to be put through a preliminary examination meant to determine each individual student's current level of learning so that they could be divided into smaller groups. I was assigned to the highest class in the school along with only two other students. The other two students, Habib and Anis, were respectively, five and six years older than me. The difference in age was due to the different standards between schools in Beirut and the schools in Shweir. I felt terribly out of place being in a class with two older boys, and was relieved when the classes broke up for a recess and I could join the boys my own age.

It took several weeks for classes to settle into a routine. Times were tough and prices were skyrocketing due to the war. Many parents had to pull their children out of school and put them to work to help them make ends meet. Each morning, I would arrive at school to hear that yet another of my schoolmates would no longer be attending classes. A main part of the routine was the twice-weekly morning Mass held in the school chapel, which was attended by both boys and girls. The older students looked forward to these occasions as they were the only times the boys and the girls got the opportunity to talk to each other. Father Hatoum conducted the Mass and Halim and Paul, along with the two nuns who taught in the girls' school, assisted.

It did not take long for the schoolwork to become routine for me. Then, one Friday in early November, an incident occurred which caused unusual excitement around the school. It was a sombre day, grey with drizzling rain, and most of the students had stayed in their classrooms during their morning break to stay warm and dry around the fireplace. Some of the older boys had gone outside to play ball and it was while we were in the schoolyard that the incident occurred. A matron, who lived a few blocks from the school, had come running out of her house and directly into the schoolyard where she singled me and one of the students playing ball, and began beating us with a shoe she held in her hand. Both of us raised our hands to try to protect ourselves from the blows, but the matron kept striking us all over our bodies and we could not extricate ourselves. Some of the boys who had been playing in the yard circled around, giggling and laughing, except for George, who dashed into the school to notify Paul of what was happening. Paul came hurrying out of the school and interceded until the matron finally relented in her attack but only after yelling and calling us a few more dirty names and slipping a few more blows around our shoulders. Once free of the attacker, we fled, shaken and trembling, into the school, to hide in our classroom. Paul stayed in the schoolyard with the matron, calming her down and attempting to find out what had caused the ruckus. After a few moments, he ordered the gawking students into the school. The students reluctantly obeyed, gossiping and speculating about what had caused the commotion until Halim shushed them.

When Paul returned to the classroom he did not offer an explanation to the students and so it was natural that rumours began to circulate around the schoolyard. Eventually, the true story came out: my friend and I had overheard Anis and Habib talking quietly to each other about a suspected romance between Paul and the matron. My friend had gone home and repeated the gossip to his mother who in turn had spread the rumour to her friends and soon the entire village was talking about the "romance" between Paul and the matron. When the matron learned about the gossip and traced it back to the two boys, she exploded and did what she felt was appropriate in the circumstances to protect her honour. Unfortunately, the matter did not end there. At the request of Father Hatoum, Paul had to resign his position for personal reasons and was forced to leave the town. The priest took over Paul's teaching duties for several weeks, until he was able to hire a new teacher from the neighbouring town of Kinchara.

A few weeks after arriving at the school, the new teacher, Antoine Al Hunud, approached the priest about staging two plays during Easter. There was a sense of general relief among the teachers when the priest approved the idea, as they felt strongly that the war had created a sombre and heavy atmosphere around the school and in the town and they hoped the plays would help lighten things up. The students were enthusiastic and ready to do whatever was necessary to help stage the plays. The teachers suggested several titles and they finally settled on the classic Arabic tale, "Forgiveness, an Arab Trait", the story of the battle of Damascus during the Ummayad's conquest, and Moliere's "Le Medecin Malgre Lui" which was translated into Arabic. Antoine started canvassing the students to see who would like to play the main roles and to his amazement found no one, except me, who wanted to tackle both main roles in each of the plays. Despite entreaties to the other students to help out and take a major role, Antoine failed to convince anyone and finally decided to let me play lead roles in both plays. Antoine encouraged each student to learn his role by heart so that we could aim to start rehearsals by the first week of February. However, long before the first week of February rolled around, to his great pleasure, Antoine noticed the boys playing their parts and shouting their lines in mock battles during the recess. We had found a new diversion, which helped distract us from the doom and gloom of the war. Antoine was sure his job as director of the plays was going to be considerably easier due to the enthusiastic role-playing he was observing during the schoolyard play. However, when rehearsals finally began, Antoine was sorely disappointed to discover that while each one knew his role by heart, recitation of the lines was in high, monotonous voices, our gestures were wooden and our arms and legs jerked around at the oddest moments. One of the students froze completely and could not utter one word and this was without even the benefit of an audience. At the end of the first week of rehearsals, Antoine was so let down, he did not know what to do and he quietly left the students in the classroom and straggled down the hall but the students shouts echoed in his ears as he walked away. Antoine was sitting on a bench in the hallway, dejectedly considering his options, when he noticed the shoes of the Mother Superior from the girls' school directly in front of him. He looked up to find Mother Marie frowning down at him. Without a word from Mother Marie, Antoine understood the problem and immediately stood up to apologize and promise that all future rehearsals would be considerably quieter. He then returned to the boys in his classroom, who had not even noticed his absence, and, with renewed energy, began to try to teach us something about acting and voice control.

Over the next three weeks, Antoine was able to arrange ten rehearsal periods and finally, on the tenth run through, began to feel hope that the plays would be ready on schedule for a passable performance.

Antoine planned to stage the two plays in the girls' school where the chapel and the classrooms could be turned into a large hall capable of seating most of the parents and neighbours. A small stage was constructed at one end of the classrooms, clothing was borrowed from family closets and the boys were taught some simple choreography. Antoine was not completely satisfied with all the arrangements, but realized that the war situation was limiting the possibilities. Father Hatoum and Mother Marie agreed to allow a full dress rehearsal for all the students, boys and girls, in one afternoon in place of classes. The dress rehearsal went off rather smoothly and Antoine began to feel some excitement building for the final performance. He noticed, that while the children enjoyed the Moliere play, they did not seem to appreciate the Arabic story. I, as the lead actor in Moliere, became an overnight celebrity in the school and the students carried tales of my performance home to their parents with an invitation to attend the performance the next day. Word of mouth proved to be effective advertising and the hall started to fill up soon after the doors were opened on Sunday afternoon. Many parents brought their neighbours or friends as well as their children and by the time the first play was ready to begin, all of the seats were full and spectators were standing at the back and along the sides of the hall. Father Hatoum said a few words of welcome and thanked Mother Marie for donating the hall, the parents for donating the costumes and Antoine and Halim for their hard work teaching, directing and producing the two plays.

The Arabic play was presented first and Habib, playing the Emir, was impressive in his robes and with his straight posture, but his voice was not strong enough to please Antoine, particularly when he was to declare, at the climax of the play, that "Forgiveness by the conquering Emirs is a true trait of the Arabs." Nevertheless, the audience greeted the declaration with whistles, stomping and a standing ovation for several minutes. When the actors were presented to the audience at the end of the play, the audience applauded them warmly. I, who had played the main villain and chieftain of one of the conquered tribes, was also applauded loudly for my acting.

When the Moliere play was presented, the audience was captivated. There were bursts of laughter throughout, but the most enthusiastic response was for me in the role of the impostor doctor. I was swept away with the audience reaction and began to improvise some of my scenes. I even slipped a large alarm clock down my pants and pointing at it I made the clock ring at will which generated a loud and prolonged cackle from the audience. When the play was over and the actors were presented to the audience, I received the loudest and warmest applause of the evening. As the audience filed out, talking and laughing, Mr. Al Hunud gathered his actors together to congratulate them for a job well done and commended me for my improvisation.

The plays, the performers and Mr. Al Hunud were the talk of the village for the next few weeks. Wherever I went, I was the object of congratulations. I found the attention delightful and much to my surprise, my nickname around Shweir became "Le Medecin".

5 Teenage Experience and Additional Schooling in Shweir

The school year in Shweir passed quickly after the plays were presented. It seemed to me that spring arrived faster than it had in Beirut and, very soon after that, it seemed the schools closed early for the summer so that the students could help their parents on their small farms and with other local activities. My first job that summer was to help my father repair the terrace walls around our fields, which had been damaged by the winter rainstorms. Next, I recruited my friends, Victor and Jamil, to help me till the vegetable farm and vineyards. It took the three of us almost two full weeks of 15-hour days to complete that job. Then, because my father had to leave again to Houran, Syria, I had to help my mother plant and irrigate the garden. I also did some simple terrace wall contracting work to earn cash to help pay for whatever the family could not produce from our fields. Other chores included gathering fallen pine needles from the nearby forests for use as fuel for the bread oven. Each loaf of bread, when baked, came out as thin as paper, and round as a full moon, about 24 inches in diameter. My mother baked the bread on a hot metal spherical pan about three feet in diameter, called the "Saj". The paper-thin bread was used to scoop up morsels of food since forks and spoons were not then commonly available nor used in the village. During my forays into the pine forests with my friends, I found myself noticing girls for the first time. There were two in particular, who were around my age and who attended the girls' side of the parish school. Both of them seemed to reciprocate my interest, but the attraction never went beyond amorous smiles as I was slated to go to work for my older cousin, Elias, who had a grocery store and café in Dhoor, in the neighbouring hills of Shweir. The store and café catered to the wealthy summer residents that fled to the mountains to escape the summer heat and humidity of Beirut. My work began each day at 5:00 AM, when I joined my cousin Habib, Elias' younger brother, and the driver, Habib Al Armani, in his truck. Together we drove to fetch ice blocks from the beer plant in Jdeideh, on the outskirts of Beirut. We would deliver the ice blocks to the grocery stores, butcher shops, hotels and residences of the rich residents of Dhoor and take a few remaining blocks to Elias' store to be retailed to his customers as they requested. The ice distribution was usually completed by about 10:00 and Habib and I would spend the rest of the day in the store selling groceries or making deliveries. We also made sandwiches, sold cold drinks and served a few customers who sat at the tables and chairs set up in front of the store. Elias liked to stay open for business until 11:00 PM and it soon became clear that with the long early hours it was too tiresome for Habib and me to "commute" between Dhoor and Shweir. The travel, one way, took at least half an hour. Elias told Habib and me that we could bring our sleeping mats up to Dhoor and sleep on the rear balcony of the store. It was a small balcony and both of us felt like sardines whenever we went to bed. After a few weeks of this routine, it became clear again that another change was required as we were not sleeping at night and were showing up to work with bleary eyes and too tired to work the full day. Habib and I made the decision this time. We decided to build ourselves a tree house in my parent's vineyard, which was only a five-minute walk from the store. We managed to build a little house in a few days and thankfully moved our sleeping mats into the new place where we found we were able to sleep to our hearts' content. The vineyard was on a hill overlooking Shweir and the surrounding villages, providing Habib and me with a spectacular view. In the morning, we could hear the roosters crowing, at night, the dogs barking and during the day and early evening, the birds singing. Frogs, butterflies, small animals and insects were everywhere. Sleeping in the tree house was invigorating and we felt we were in heaven.

Summer passed quickly. Soon Elias was telling us that his business had slowed down for the season and he would no longer need our help and services. We were sad but there was nothing to be done and we returned home, regretfully giving up our tree house.

The wheat crop in Lebanon was meagre that summer and the price of wheat began to skyrocket as people began to hoard supplies. The government announced it would buy up the entire summer's crop at a fixed price and would then distribute the crop to its citizens in accordance with the size of each family. The price was fixed at about 50 per cent of the market price. The government appointed distributors for each village and gave coupons to the people throughout Lebanon to purchase wheat. Elias was appointed distributor for Shweir and he asked Habib and me to help him look after the wheat warehouse. Elias' sister, Linda, looked after the books. The warehouse work was tiresome as it involved weighing and loading the wheat for the customers. When it was not busy, Habib and I would either play with the two cats that inhabited the warehouse or slide down the bags of wheat. Generally, the wheat distribution went smoothly except when someone would complain their share was inadequate because their grandparents had moved in with them. Elias would have to explain that it was only the secretary of the municipality who could increase the number of coupons per family and while this explanation satisfied most people, some would insist on dragging Elias off to their homes to verify their story.

After a summer of hard work, I was glad to see school reopen in October. I returned to school along with most of the teachers and students. However, some of the older students did not enrol. They were working instead to help their parents provide for their families. The fall was unusually cold and humid and many of the students came down with the flu. I picked up the virus and passed it on to my entire family. My father, back from his work in Houran, was hardest hit. His fever and symptoms were so severe that my mother consulted our relative and neighbour Imm Dawood for advice. Imm Dawood was the oldest and supposedly the wisest woman in the neighbourhood. After Imm Dawood had listened to my father's cough she announced that he needed "Hjabat", a practice involving applying suction cups to the patient's back. Imm Dawood said she would go home to get the necessary instruments and come back after dinner. My sisters loved Imm Dawood who was also known for her children's stories and were terribly excited to hear she would be back in the evening. When Imm Dawood reappeared, with her husband, her daughter Zalfa and several neighbours in tow, they gathered around my father's bed and my sisters, my brother and I also crowded around to see what would happen. While Imm Dawood was preparing herself she began to tell us the story of Jiha, his son and their donkey. We laughed the hardest when Jiha wound up carrying the donkey on his back in order to satisfy his critical neighbours. Once the story was finished, we were ordered to bed so that Imm Dawood could begin her ministrations. I was the only one allowed to stay up to watch the procedure.

Imm Dawood asked Ward Imm Karim, my mother, to bring a candle, a cup of olive oil and some scrap paper. She asked my father to lie down on his stomach on his bed and to clear the clothes off his back. Then Imm Dawood lit the candle and took a small piece of paper, which she rolled into a tube and held over the flame. When the paper was burning well, she placed it in one of the special glasses that she brought with her and then placed the glass cup upside down on my father's back. In a few seconds the burning paper was extinguished and my father's skin and flesh were sucked up into the glass as though being vacuumed up. Imm Dawood repeated the procedure several times until my father's back was swollen and as red as a monkey's bottom. She then heated the olive oil in a ladle and rubbed the warm oil over my father's back until his skin was shiny and glowing. That was the entire procedure and once it was over, my father was supposed to feel better and shake off the flu shortly thereafter. My father turned over in his bed, thanked Imm Dawood and assured her that he already felt relief from his symptoms and maybe he would even be able to go to work the next day. Imm Dawood discouraged him from returning to work just yet, saying she thought he might need one more session before he would be back on his feet. My father agreed, settled back into bed and asked my mother to serve coffee and cake to Imm Dawood and the other neighbours who had come over to watch Imm Dawood's work. My mother invited everyone to sit down and enjoy some cards as well and they were soon into a game of Trump. As for my father, he felt much better the next day, but it took an additional three sessions of Hjabat before he was able to completely shake off his illness.

The adults in the village generally entertained themselves with cards, singing and playing the "Ood", the Lebanese guitar, gambling and duelling with colloquial poetry as the weapon of choice. The favourite card game was Trump and some of the villagers were so good at it that they had fans that would come around just for the pleasure of watching them play. The presence of the fans helped create a raucous atmosphere whenever Trump was being played. I remember many a Sunday afternoon when the players and their entourage gathered on the flat roof of my grandfather's home which was easily accessible and centrally located in the village. The bolstering, shouting and laughter of the players would attract many of their fans to join them and participate in the friendly, hilarious teasing and enliven the fun and raucous entertaining atmosphere.

Another favoured form of entertainment was for several friends to gather at someone's home, to sing traditional songs and ballads then move on from house to house entertaining those who were prepared to listen to them or join them in the singing. One of my favourite entertainments was to listen to my uncle Amin mimic my father and others of his friends and acquaintances. Amin was so good at it, that many of those present would laugh their heads off even when they were being mimicked themselves!

I remembered December that year as being a particularly exciting time at the Nasser home. My mother was due to deliver her sixth baby and one evening my father asked me, with some urgency in his voice, to go and tell the "Khourieh", the midwife, that my mother, Ward, was ready to deliver her baby. In the meantime, my father called Imm Dawood and Imm Nassib to look after Ward. They put my brother, Fadlallah, to bed and my sisters, Najla, Jouliette, and Karimeh, to work cleaning the house, boiling up a huge amount of water and preparing the bed for my mother. Imm Dawood asked my father to pull two chickens from the coop and to slaughter them so that she could cook them for Ward. It was the village tradition to feed chicken soup to new mothers for two weeks after giving birth, as this would ensure plenty of breast milk for the new baby. My father did as he was asked. He picked out two plump chickens, slit their throats and left them in the yard to bleed to death before they would be cleaned in hot water and cooked according to a special recipe.

The midwife arrived after supper, inspected the bed, the clothing for the baby and all the accessories needed for delivery. She was pleased with what she saw but she ordered Imm Karim to bed and sent the children to stay next door. Her orders were reluctantly complied with and only Najla was finally allowed to stay behind in case she was needed to help find things around the house. At the neighbours', my sisters, my brother and I stayed up late playing and roasting oak acorns in the fireplace. We slashed the skin of each acorn to relieve the pressure that would develop while the nut was being roasted. The occasional acorn was not properly slashed and would explode, creating a racket that sent the children into paroxysms of laughter and excitement. The roasted acorns had a sweet taste but could produce bellyaches and lots of gas if consumed in great quantities.

Early the next morning, Najla came over to wake aunt Haifa, her family, and her brothers and sisters and announce that a baby girl had been born in the wee hours of the morning. She had been named "Noha". Literally translated, it meant this is the last female princess that would be born in our family! The birth had gone smoothly and mother and child were fine and resting at home. My siblings and I became wild with excitement and wanted to go home immediately to see the new baby, but Haifa Imm Elias calmed us down and convinced us to let our mother and the new baby rest until lunchtime. We reluctantly agreed and settled back into bed, not without some squirming. When the lunch hour finally rolled around, we trooped home together, we kissed our mother and held the new baby for a few seconds each. We ate lunch, and after lunch, the neighbours began to come over to see the new baby and wish mother and child good health, happiness and the blessings of the Lord. They brought with them gifts of fruits, sweets, food or baby clothes. The adults were offered coffee and cigarettes and "Harrow Esboh", bread fried with butter and dipped in molasses, while the children were each given a handful of sugar-coated dried chickpeas.

After a few days, life for the Nasser family returned to normal. The children would get up early, have breakfast and do their chores then go to school. Najla now had the additional job of washing the baby's potty and "Sciaback" which were used to collect the urine and feces of the baby as she slept in her crib. The sciaback looked like an enlarged spoon that fit over the urethra or penis of a new baby and carried the baby's urine through the hollow handle to the potty, which sat in a special depression at the bottom of the crib. Both gadgets were made of glazed pottery so that they could be washed with soap and hot water and kept clean and odourless. Najla would empty the potty at the outhouse, which was in the yard next to the storm gutter. Whenever a good rainstorm hit the town, the storm water would be diverted to pass through the pit of the outhouse to carry the sewage to a drainage ditch and from there to the outskirts of town. As the town was located on the side of a hill, there was good drainage for a fast flow of wastewater. What a sight and mixture of awful odours when all the neighbours decided to take advantage of a good steady rain.

The war was creating fear of famine in the village; many of the elders in the village had survived the First World War and remembered their deprivation and the scarcity of provisions. The villagers were urged to economize and to plant every nook and cranny with wheat and other grains. My father had to go again to Houran to look for work and he urged me to look after the small farm and to act as the man of the house. I was asked to make sure there were stocks on hand to feed the family and to assist my mother in buying provisions.

To cut expenses, the family began to cut each other's hair at home. I ducked out of this event, afraid that my mother or sisters would mangle my hair, and instead arranged with two of my classmates that we would cut each other's hair. The boys waved around their scissors and combs and assured each other that we knew what we were doing, but the results showed otherwise. All three boys had wild cuts, which gave our heads the appearance of newly plowed fields. Our mothers were horrified and each boy was ordered to the barber for repair work before we would be allowed to make an appearance at school the next day.

The same two schoolmates, Elias and Wadih, and I had much better results when we helped each other till the family fields. This time, our efforts were applauded as we completed our tasks in time for our mothers to plant and seed the fields. Unfortunately, a heavy rainstorm washed out one of the terrace walls in our field. I decided to undertake the repair of the wall myself. It was going to involve a lot of heavy labour and common sense knowledge to place and reinforce the stones so that they would withstand the pressures of heavy, wet soil piled to a depth of two meters. Mortar was not used on the terrace walls. Hence, it was tricky to lay out the stones in an appropriate thickness to ensure the wall could resist the high soil pressure. When I had built up the wall to the half way point, Simaan, our next-door neighbour, came by to look at my work. Simaan was impressed and praised me for my efforts, which made me happy and confident that I could continue and finish the repair job.

When I was on my way home after my work on the terrace wall, I found a crowd gathered in front of Jiryes' house. I asked Najm, a school friend and a cousin who was standing in the crowd, what was going on and quickly learned that Jiryes and his wife were in the middle of a fight. Their four children had become frightened and fled to a neighbour's house. The neighbour, Nazira, came out of the house and went into Jiryes' house to try and calm the parents down, without success. Instead, the argument got louder and more violent, with dishes flying and striking the walls. Nazira came out of the house, shielding Mrs. Jiryes with her arm, and led the frightened woman to her house to join the children. Jiryes appeared at the door, in an apparent attempt to follow the two women, but he was obviously drunk and unable to walk. Jiryes' brother Ayyoub appeared in the doorway behind Jiryes and dragged him back into the house. Things then quieted down and the crowd dispersed, some laughing, some shaking their heads in dismay. I went home and told my mother what I had seen and she told me the fights happened occasionally, whenever Jiryes lost money gambling and as a consequence would have too much to drink. I was a little shook up by the family fight I had witnessed, but I forgot the troubles when my mother told me we would be having a special dessert that evening in appreciation of my work on the terrace wall. My mother had made fig jam in melted butter and roasted pine fruit, a special treat that we did not see too often in these hard times. It is really a very delicious treat that I recommend to all those with a sweet tooth.

As summer approached and the weather got milder, some of the Australian soldiers who were stationed in the village could be seen swimming occasionally in the river reservoir belonging to Abu Dawood. One warm Saturday afternoon, I asked my mother for permission to go swimming in the river reservoir. My mother was reluctant to allow me to go on my own but I assured her that I would not swim until some of the Australian soldiers were also swimming as they were reputed to be good swimmers and lifeguards. When my mother finally agreed, I rounded up my friend Sami and together we made our way to the river where we found three Australian soldiers already swimming. We tried to talk to the soldiers but we could not speak English and the soldiers could speak neither Arabic nor French. Nevertheless, we smiled at each other and the atmosphere was friendly.

Sami and I agreed that we would swim one at a time and if anything went wrong, the one on the riverbank would extend a branch to the one in the water to help him out safely. There were a number of branches and tree trunks lying next to the reservoir, which Abu Dawood was using to repair the roof of his patio where he would nap when it was too hot to do anything else. I was the first to dive into the water, as I was supposedly the one with more experience. I hit the water with a large splash and once in the water opened my eyes to see where I was. However, my dive had muddied the water and I could not see a thing. I panicked and tried to work my way back to the riverbank, but I was having trouble staying afloat and began to swallow water. One of the Australian soldiers noticed me struggling and dove in to drag me to the side of the reservoir and out of the water. Once on dry ground, I threw up and began to shiver, looking tired and sick. The soldier wrapped me in his blanket to warm me up and steady my nerves and it was around fifteen minutes before I felt well enough to try and thank the soldier for his help. Once I was on my feet again, Sami and I returned home to find our mothers sitting in the shade in front of the Nasser home. When we told our mothers what had happened, their emotions alternated between worry for our safety and gratitude to the soldiers for their help. The story soon spread through the village and friends and neighbours began to drop by to see me and make sure I was fine. The next day, there was a village religious feast and procession in honour of St. Sauveur, the patron saint of our church. My classmates and I joined in the procession and the priest, during his sermon and prayers, thanked the Lord and the Australians for saving me.

During spring the government announced municipal elections were to be held throughout Lebanon for the first time ever. Shweir was engulfed in election fever. The villagers began to talk about the election and its importance as if it were the answer for all the difficulties brought by the war. Groups began to form in the town with the express purpose of choosing candidates based on religious and familial affiliations. My father, Wadih, became active in the Christian group and was instrumental in nominating Michel, a family member, his friend and next-door neighbour, as a candidate for the village district. A few weeks prior to the Election Day, Sabah, also known as Imm Assad, the matriarch of the Khenaisser family, appeared at our doorstep. She had come to solicit my father's support for her son, Assad, who was running against Michel. As she stood talking to my father, Imm Assad held the new baby Noha, rocking her gently in her arms while she presented her arguments in support of her son, Assad. My father advised Imm Assad that he and the whole family had already agreed at a family gathering to support Michel and he did not see how he could change his mind now and vote for Assad even though he liked his cousin Assad very much. Imm Assad argued that nobody would know how Wadih voted and he could still pretend that he had voted for Michel. My father, holding his temper in check, vehemently responded that his honour, integrity and faithfulness would not be compromised by such behaviour. He had been raised to respect people and to adhere to principles and what Imm Assad was proposing went against everything he believed in. Imm Assad herself became visibly angry at my father's words and her face flushed bright red. She bent over, laid the new baby on the floor and turned on her heels and left the house without saying good-bye. Emotions were high and the baby reacted with shrieks that could be heard two houses away.

Two weeks later, Fathers Hatoum, Elias and Maroun, as well as Reverend Sedrassi, the four religious leaders in Shweir, agreed among themselves to call for a strike in the town and its suburbs to protest the inadequate distribution of wheat from the central government. Each religious leader, during his Sunday sermon, asked his parishioners to gather on Monday morning at 10:00 AM in the town square in front of the Greek Catholic church. From there, the villagers would march as a group behind the four religious leaders to the Municipal building. A large number of students were among the gathered protesters on Monday morning and they were especially enthusiastic in leading the chant "We want wheat, we want flour, we want to eat, we are hungry." When the protesters arrived at the Municipal building they were met by the Chief of Police, who promised the crowd that he would convey their demands to the authorities. The holy men were not satisfied, however, and they demanded to speak to the President of the Republic on the telephone to make him appreciate the seriousness of the situation. The following negotiations with the Chief of Police were noisy and emotional, but after fifteen minutes, the Chief yielded to the holy men and led them into the Municipal building where they eventually reached the President by telephone. While Father Hatoum was on the phone with the President, Reverend Sedrassi led the crowd in cheers and calls and answers.

"Do you want a municipal election?" and the villagers responded with a roar, "NO!"

"What do you want?"

"We want wheat, we want to eat, and we are hungry!"

The President could hear the crowd over the phone line in Beirut and promised Father Hatoum that he would order the Director of Supplies to send more supplies of wheat to the village immediately.

The day after the demonstration, the municipal secretary announced that the government was sending five truckloads of wheat to Shweir. As word spread through the town, the excitement grew as people began to realize that the President was coming to deliver the wheat. Excitement grew into frenzy and plans were made to hold a rally for the President so the townspeople could express their appreciation for his help. The scheduled delivery day was a Sunday and a public Mass was also planned in the town square to thank God for His blessings and to pray for the long life of the President. The townspeople began to gather at 10:00 in the morning and soon after heard the roar of the police motorcycles and the wail of sirens as the President's motorcade wound its way up the mountain to Shweir, followed by five trucks of wheat. The townspeople cheered wildly. When the President finally arrived and got out of his car to greet the mayor, he was invited to join the celebration of the Mass. The President agreed and his bodyguards and the secret police stationed themselves strategically around him in the square. When the Mass was over the President addressed the gathered people to wish them well and promised there would be no further shortages of wheat. The crowd clapped and cheered but in the silence that followed one squeaky voice was heard proclaiming that the President was overweight and needed to diet to spare some wheat for the poor. When people looked around to see who was speaking, they saw me and my friends standing together in front of the butcher shop. One of the presidential guards and a member of the secret police came over to march me away from the crowd and over to the local police station where they interrogated me to see if I were involved in some sort of a plot against the President. I was really scared and trembling and all I could say was that I had learned in my school hygiene class that overweight people should diet to improve their health. The local police chief who was observing the interrogation burst into laughter and told the President's men that the hygiene instructor was a health nut and they should ignore this incident. After some private discussion with the chief of police, the men from Beirut relented and let me go, but not before giving me a good shake and strictly advising me to keep my thoughts about public figures to myself.

That evening, I told my parents about the incident. They were shocked and warned me to be careful in the future and not to comment in public about government employees, as they were known to be protective of their positions and were not afraid to use their power to assert their influence over ordinary citizens. My father said to me that as a matter of principle, if you have nothing good to say about someone, then it is best not to say anything at all.

At night, I woke up twice from scary dreams involving the police. In one dream, the police had surrounded our home in order to arrest and jail me for insulting the President. Thankfully, I had to get up early the next morning to go to the Massarah, which saved me from worse nightmares. The Massarah is a small outdoor plant where villagers extract molasses "dibs" from grapes. Today was my family's turn to press our grapes. My father and uncle Sabih had already left for the vineyard to pick up the grapes and haul them to the Massarah. By the time I arrived, I found my uncle already pressing the grapes with his bare feet, and squeezing the juice out so that it drained into a large metal container placed below an open ditch. I took off my shoes, rinsed my feet with water and joined my uncle in the rock-lined pit where the grapes were dumped. Together, we stamped our feet and strode back and forth from one end of the pit to the other. Sabih laughed at my technique and tried to teach me how to squeeze the grapes systematically with feet placed closely together, allowing the juice to ooze out between the toes. The pit was about ten feet square and tiled with smooth stones to help minimize the loss of the grape juice. There were three pits in the Massarah to meet the village demand. However, all three pits led to one brass pot, five feet in diameter and four feet deep. The grape juice would be heated to boiling in this pot to make the molasses. The Massarah was open 24 hours a day during the last three weeks of September. Grapes normally were ripe at that time of the summer and a festival atmosphere enveloped the village during the three weeks. Adults and children would gather to roast potatoes and onions in the fire burning beneath the brass pot and to skim off the foam from the surface of the molasses to eat with bread. Songs were sung, games were played and there was plenty of excitement. The owner of the Massarah was paid with ten per cent of the molasses produced for using his equipment. He was the only person in town who had built a Massarah and he had sensibly located it near the village vineyards. During the three weeks it was in operation, the fire and smoke from the Massarah could be seen from anywhere in the village. The scent of hot grape molasses, roasted potatoes, onions, garlic and eggplant intermingled to cause everyone who could smell the aroma to suddenly feel the urge to eat. The foam off the top of the boiling grapes was uniquely irresistible to the village children who could be found clustered around the brass pot at all times of the day. The firing up of the Massarah signalled to the children the end of the summer and, for many, the resumption of school.

I did not return to school that year as my parents could not afford to pay the tuition and they were too embarrassed to ask to have the fees waived, even though it was accepted practice and easily granted. Instead, I began to assist my father, Abu Karim, in managing the small family farm and at whatever other work my father could line up. My father was planning to place bids on two municipal jobs and I was also involved in helping him put the bids together. One contract would be to collect fees from the peddlers who sold their wares door to door and the other was to collect and dispose of the village garbage. In a procedure similar to an auction, bids were to be placed openly in the municipal office at the end of November. On the morning of the bidding, the municipal secretary, Jamil Moujaes, began the proceedings with the garbage contract. Zaid Al Hourani placed the first bid. Silence reigned, as it seemed no one was prepared to bid against Zaid. As the municipal secretary was about to make the final call for bids, I shouted out to enter the competition. The secretary smiled at me and thanked me for the bid but went on to say that my lack of experience would disqualify me from the bidding. My father put his arm around my shoulders and squeezed me close to whisper that Zaid badly needed the work and it would be best not to bid against him. I did not understand but knew I could not go against my father's wishes and so I quietly agreed to let my father decide when to speak up. Soon after, the municipal secretary opened the bidding for the Hisbey. My father actively bid for the contract, as did several men in the village, but Nabil kept topping each bid until everybody else had to drop out, including my father, and the contract was awarded to Nabil. On our way home after the auction, my father and Najib, our relative and neighbour, began to discuss the bidding. Najib felt that nobody could outbid the Ajroudeh Nabil, who had already won the contract for each of the preceding five years. I asked Najib what was the meaning of Ajroudeh and Najib explained that it was a cross between a male and female who cannot grow a beard or ever get married. This was a new word for me and I had to ask my father if there really were such a thing. My father explained that there really were strange things occurring in nature and one good example was the mule. I felt confused but decided not to pursue the conversation, as Najib seemed to be laughing at my questions. However, Najib was not a hard man and when he realized how upset I was that he and my father had not won any of the contracts, Najib suggested I come and help raise Najib's silk cocoons (kazz). I got my father's permission and happily followed Najib home, curious to see the silk cocoons.

The first job Najib gave me was to feed shredded mulberry leaves to the Shranek, the white caterpillar worms. The worms were placed on round bamboo trays, four feet in diameter that were kept stacked on shelves in a dark room. The worms' existence consisted of munching on mulberry leaves, growing corpulent and entombing themselves in the white silk cocoons which they spun around themselves. I was excited to learn about the marvel of metamorphosis although the process followed by Najib would not allow all the cocoons to develop into actual butterflies. Once the cocoons had been spun, Najib would gather the majority of the cocoons and drop them into vats of boiling water to kill the worms so that he would remove the silk threads for spinning and subsequent manufacturing into silk cloth. However, Najib would allow some of the cocoons to complete their life cycle and become butterflies that would then lay eggs and start the cycle all over again.

Najib had a son who was five years older than me. Anis and I got to be friends while I helped with the worms and Anis suggested to me that I join the wrestling club that Anis was coordinating. The club was made up of boys my age and a few years older that met every Tuesday from 4:00 to 6:00 PM when they would receive training and instructions from Anis and the head trainer, whose name was Mikhail. The clubhouse was in an old, dark, one-room house near a general store in the village. Almost no light could get into the room as there was no window, nor was there air circulation and the room smelled badly from years of sweat. On my first Tuesday I found five other boys my age stripped down to their underwear, gathered around Mikhail, who was showing off his well-developed muscles to the group. Mikhail asked Anis to flex his muscles for the boys and promised them that after a few months of hard work with the two trainers the boys would have developed similar muscles. The boys were suitably impressed and eager to do whatever they were instructed to do. I kept attending for many weeks, until one day Anis appeared without Mikhail. At the end of the session, Anis gathered us boys together and told us we needed to ensure that our penises would grow at the same rate as the rest of our muscles. The way to ensure this was to apply, several times, enough milk from fig leaves directly to our penises. As some fig trees were growing at the side of the clubhouse, Anis told us to wait inside and he would get some leaves to demonstrate. He brought back into the clubhouse several leaves he had plucked from a tree and showed us the milky liquid that was oozing out of the stem. Nobody questioned Anis' recommendation and each boy eagerly applied the milky liquid to his penis. Soon after, each one of us could feel a harsh burning sensation and swelling of our penis, especially under the movable skin. Now the questions started, but Anis assured us that this sensation was due to the muscles growing in our penises. We quietly got dressed and headed home for dinner but by the time we got home, we were all rocking from one side to the other, in an attempt to keep our penises from touching our underwear or thighs in an attempt to minimize the pain which had become excruciating. When I got home, my mother noticed my strange and apparently painful walking and after many pointed questions she managed to extract the truth from me. She immediately made me strip off my clothes and sit in a large pail of hot, soapy water and later applied talcum powder to the sensitive skin. Then Ward, my mother, marched off to complain to Selma, Anis' mother, about this kafuffle. Although their meeting began with some heated words, my mother soon learned that Anis had suffered through the same experience a few months earlier and soon the two mothers were laughing hysterically together.

The days passed by uneventfully and I continued to help Najib until a friend of the family opened a small café whose main business was to cater to the Australian forces camping in Dhoor, the neighbouring hills of Shweir. Tannous, the café proprietor, asked me if I would like to work as a waiter in the café where he promised I would get lots of tips which would make up my wages instead of a salary. Neither Tannous nor any of his waiters spoke English so there were many miscommunications between the soldiers and the waiters. The café served only eggs, chips and beer and it was fun for me and my co-workers to be on the frontlines of the language clashes. One day one of the soldiers, obviously unhappy with what had been placed in front of him, threw his egg sandwich to the ground where it was snapped up by Tannous' dog. The soldier left the café in a huff without paying. A few weeks later, Tannous quietly closed the café.

But I had had a taste of the excitement provided by dealing with the soldiers. I made an effort to learn a few words of English and then started to peddle chocolate bars, peanuts, and gum to the soldiers. One day, one of the soldiers told me that it was his birthday and he wanted to treat his friends by giving them each a chocolate bar. He asked me for ten bars then told me that he did not have enough money to pay for everything that day and said if I came back in two days and asked for him personally, Charlie Chaplin, he would pay the price in full. I agreed to the deal as I had been treated fairly by most of the soldiers. Two days later, I returned to the camp and looked around for Charlie. I couldn't see him anywhere, so I went to the mess hall and asked the cashier about Charlie Chaplin. The cashier and his assistant roared with laughter and once they had calmed down explained to me who Charlie Chaplin was. They seemed to enjoy the joke so much that they paid the outstanding account to me and I returned home with a pocket full of change and a smile on my face at the soldiers' kindness and delightful sense of humour.

As time passed, I learned that some of the soldiers were selling blankets and gas tins on the black market to some of the local shopkeepers and to one of the municipal officers. This gave me the idea that I could do the same thing. I approached one of the soldiers and he was amenable and we worked out a deal together. I was to meet the soldier one night near the church in order to close the deal. While waiting for the soldier, the priest who was leaving his apartment to visit some of the neighbours, spotted me behind the church. The priest walked over to me and solemnly told me to go home right away before the devil appeared to frighten the life out of me. I rushed home, terrified that the devil might follow me from the churchyard.

That same evening, my father was entertaining some male neighbours over a game of cards while their wives were in the kitchen with my mother Ward, preparing special snacks. One favourite snack, "Harrow esboh" was made by frying small pieces of bread in butter and then dipping the bread in molasses. Frying pine nuts with fig jam in butter made another snack, my favourite. Also, the women prepared a mixture of molasses, flour, oil and baking soda, which they baked in the oven. As the evening progressed, the card players became louder and more boisterous. In the middle of a particularly loud round of cards there came a knock at the door. My father opened the door and was surprised to find the municipal policeman and a member of the military police standing at the door. He invited them in and politely asked them what they wanted. The policeman said they were looking for me and they intended to search the house for military blankets and gas tins. My father told them that I had already been in bed for several hours but they were welcome to search the house. The policeman seemed surprised to find that, indeed, I was curled up in my bed, although not asleep, and was not in fact out trying to buy blankets and gas tins as they had been told. They apologized to my father and left and the party resumed where it had been interrupted. My sisters pounced on me once the policeman had left and demanded to know what mischief I was involved in. I denied that I had been up to anything at all and went to my mother to make sure she believed me. Ward seemed satisfied with my innocence and gave me some fig dessert before sending me back to bed. The dessert tasted especially delicious to me and I was flooded with a feeling of relief and sent out a prayer of thanks to the priest for chasing me home before the devil had got hold of me.

6 Teenager at International College in Beirut

The next morning, over breakfast, I broke down in tears. My parents were surprised at the outbreak, which was unusual behaviour for me, and began to question me to discover the reason for my tears. Wadih and Ward thought it was probably a result of the policeman's visit the night before and tried to tell me that I had nothing to worry about, but their words did nothing to calm down my sobbing. Eventually, with my parents' prodding, I stopped crying and was able to begin to talk through my sniffles. I looked at each of my parents in turn and in a firm voice told them I wanted to return to school and continue on to university. Ward and Wadih were surprised but pleased at my ambition, but they knew they did not have the money to pay for my tuition. They promised to help me in any way they could, but this year there was nothing extra for my schooling. Perhaps next year would be better. I felt better at hearing their words of support and thanked them for their encouragement. I then finished my breakfast quickly, still occasionally sniffling, and went out to do my chores.

Later that day, I received a message from Father Hatoum, to come to the parish school. I was uncertain of the reason for the summons, but I went at the appointed time and was greeted by the priest with a wide smile. Father Hatoum asked me to sit down and after a few pleasantries were exchanged told me that the elementary teacher had decided to quit teaching and to enter a monastery. Father Hatoum invited me to teach the elementary students for the remainder of the term and I quickly agreed to take on the responsibility as I knew this would be my chance to make some money for my own education. Father Hatoum was clearly pleased with my decision and asked me if I could start the next day. He went on to say the school could only pay me 15 Lebanese pounds per month, which was approximately equal to $5.00. I said this amount would be satisfactory to me, since I never made that much money before, and added I would report to work the next day at 7:00 AM. The priest said that was fine and he would then outline my new duties. We shook hands and I hurried home to tell my parents the good news.

The next morning, I arrived at the school at 6:30 and was surprised to find the priest already in his office. Father Hatoum welcomed me with his usual wide smile and told me I would be in charge of classroom #2, which had about forty students in five different grades. My duties would be to teach and supervise the five grades, to give them homework, correct their work for the next day, and to supervise the students during their recess. If any of the students got out of hand, I was to send them over to classroom #1 where Father Hatoum would deal with them.

While we were talking in the priest's office, the school bell rang and the students began to file into their classrooms. Father Hatoum took me in to my new classroom and introduced me to the students as their new teacher. As soon as the priest left the room, an unusual quiet wave of reaction passed through the class followed by laughter. I joined in the laughter and when everyone had quieted down again, I pointed to an Arabic proverb framed on a wooden plaque hung on the wall and read it aloud to my class:

"Teaching the young is like sculpting in stone."

I intoned in a firm voice.

"That's what your father does every day!" one of the older students shouted out from the back corner. I smiled and responded: "If you or any one in this class is not serious enough and neglects your studies, you will be working in the stone quarries for the rest of your lives." After that, the rest of the day passed quietly and quickly for me.

Teaching five grades in the same room proved to be quite a challenge for me, especially as I had to deal with the two eldest students who had been my playmates before I started teaching. Jamil and Tony were friendly and well-behaved most of the time, but they would occasionally act up and play tricks on me. One morning, when all the students had been seated, I opened my desk drawer to pull out a pencil. I was startled when a frog leaped out of the drawer and landed on my desk, croaking and twitching. As I made a grab for the frog, it leaped off the desk and began to hop around the room, creating chaos in the classroom, until one of the students finally caught the frog and put it out the door. Another time, Tony brought a bird into the classroom and let it loose while the class was practicing a hymn for the Easter service. Again, the class was brought to a standstill until the bird was caught and released outside. I then told the class the bird was a good omen, signaling the arrival of spring with its promise of renewal of life.

When I had made up my mind to pursue higher education I did not realize there was a difference between high school and university. I learned the difference after inquiring of my friend, Anis, how best to pursue my goal. Anis and his parents lived near the summer home of Professor Van Devan of the American University of Beirut (AUB). Professor Van Devan had been instrumental in helping Anis become a part-time student at the university and finding a job on campus. At first, Anis was a little reluctant to introduce me to the Professor. He finally relented but only after warning me to avoid going to Professor Van Devan's office at the AUB and to never say a word to a soul that the Professor was homosexual. Then Anis had to explain in detail to me how the Professor had lured him into his office on the pretext of showing him some pictures of old dinosaurs and as they stood near the window to get better light, the Professor had moved in close to Anis and started rubbing up against Anis' buttocks. Anis had hastily declined the Professor's advances and he wanted to make sure I did not fall into the same trap. I was taken aback by the information and, after some thought, decided I would look for alternative sources of help for my education.

My grandmother Nabiha and my aunts and uncle came from Beirut in the spring to celebrate Easter with us. Soon after they arrived, I told them of my intention to return to Beirut to attend the university and I asked if they knew of anyone who could help me reach my goal. Nabiha volunteered to intercede for me with Mrs. Dodge, the wife of the president of the AUB. Mrs. Dodge regularly hired Nabiha to sew and make alterations to her formal dresses and to sew formal and casual dresses for her maids. My Grandma told me to come to Beirut next week and she would take me with her to meet and talk to Mrs. Dodge. I was excited and delighted with the offer and agreed to go down to Beirut during the Easter holidays.

The next Tuesday, I took the bus to Beirut and after picking up my grandmother at her home, the two of us rode the tramway to Ras Beirut where the university was located. The tramway was a cherished experience for me. I marvelled at the plush upholstered benches reserved for the first class passengers and compared them to the hard oakwood benches in second class. The tramway seemed to hurtle down its steel rails, vibrating and squealing as it turned corners. It took about half an hour to reach the main gates of the AUB where Sitto Nabiha and I were greeted by the guard who asked us to wait while he reported our arrival to Mrs. Dodge. I stood back to admire the heavy, ornate iron doors that swung open to allow bicycles and pedestrians onto the campus grounds. As we waited, the clock in the tower of the College building struck eleven, with a loud, clear sound that reverberated through my body. After a few moments, the guard returned and ushered Nabiha and me down the path to the president's house. I was struck by the beauty of the campus, which housed beautiful, large, stone buildings of Arabesque architecture, tall palm trees, rose bushes and shrubs overrun with all sorts of blossoms that I had not seen before. The paths and roads were clean and I could see all around me the Mediterranean, the luxurious St. George hotel and the Sunnine Mountain, which was capped with snow. I felt elated in those surroundings and I could barely breathe from hope and anticipation.

The president's house was surrounded by a beautiful garden in full bloom. The overwhelming atmosphere was one of serenity, peace, soothing fragrance and joy. Nabiha led the way to the back gate, which opened into the kitchen courtyard. Upon sounding the bell, an elderly maid came to the gate and let us in, calling out, "Ahlan wa sahlan, Nabiha." The maid and Nabiha embraced and Nabiha introduced me as her grandson. We were then directed to seat ourselves in chairs arranged under the palm trees in the courtyard. After a few moments, Mrs. Dodge appeared and came up to greet Nabiha warmly in fluent Arabic, but with a cute accent. She was a tall, graceful and handsome woman with an imposing presence that inspired respect. She sat down and ordered coffee to be served to the adults and lemonade for me. Then she began to discuss some work she wanted done as soon as possible. After a few moments, Nabiha smiled at me, and then said to Mrs. Dodge that she needed to ask a favour. Nabiha explained that I was her grandson and wanted to study at the university but neither my parents nor grandparents could help me financially. Nabiha went on to say that she hoped Mrs. Dodge could help me find a job at the university so that I could pay for my education myself.

Mrs. Dodge frowned slightly, then began to describe in great detail how much it would cost for tuition, books, room and board and pocket money, finishing her list by estimating I would need US$2,000.00 per year, or the equivalent of 6,000.00 Lebanese pounds. She glanced at me and stated it would be impossible for a person to earn that amount of money, even if he were granted substantial scholarships. Mrs. Dodge told Nabiha and me that the young professors at the university earned about $2,000.00 per year and she did not see how I could hope to earn anywhere near that amount. Nabiha bent forward in her seat and speaking intently responded that I was extremely hardworking, anxious to attend university and would do well in my studies.

Mrs. Dodge sat up even straighter in her chair and in a firm, commanding voice put an end to the conversation by stating, "Ya Nabiha, the university is for the sons of princes, sheiks and the children of wealthy families from the Arab states. It is simply not possible for you to hope for your grandson to enter the university."

Her words came as a blow to me, but did not completely dash my hopes as I knew very well that Anis' family was not any better off than my own and Anis was attending the AUB. I spoke up and reiterated that I would work extremely hard and thought that with the help of a loan that I would pay back after graduating I should be able to make my way. Mrs. Dodge responded that I would do better to learn my father's trade and work as a stonemason. Her words silenced Nabiha and me, the coldness of her tone practically taking our breath away. After politely thanking Mrs. Dodge for her time, Nabiha and I left the courtyard, silent and broken-hearted. We did not speak as we walked across the campus to the main gate. Then, Sitto Nabiha, sensing my anguish, told me she needed a drink and gave me money to get two glasses of lemonade from the stand set up near the main gate. As we stood there, waiting for the tramway and drinking the sweet/sour drink, the vendor began to play a soothing tune on his brass cups, to attract customers and entertain those standing nearby. The lemonade soothed my dry mouth, but I remained lost in deep thought, trying to imagine my next step. Despite the shattering disappointment of our meeting with Mrs. Dodge, I remained absolutely certain that I would find a way to continue my education.

The tramway arrived after a few minutes and I and Sitto Nabiha made it home in time for Nabiha to prepare dinner. In the meantime, I busied myself cleaning the yard around the apartment building. When dinner was ready and the family sat down to eat, I described our meeting with Mrs. Dodge to my uncle and aunts. They commiserated with me but encouraged me not to give up. Then my aunt Marie spoke up, saying that she would be sewing for Mrs. Joseph Haddad, who was the wife of the director of the AUB summer high school, which was located next to the main campus. She invited me to come with her tomorrow to meet Mrs. Haddad and to see if I could get some guidance from her. My spirits shot back up at hearing this suggestion and I quickly agreed to Marie's idea. I was too excited to fall asleep until late in the night, and I was the first one up the next morning, dressed and ready to go before Marie had even got out of bed.

Marie and I were on the tramway by 7:00 AM, joining in the rush of people heading to school and jobs. We arrived at Mrs. Haddad's home forty-five minutes later where we were greeted by the maid and ushered around the back to the verandah patio where the sewing machine was kept. Mrs. Haddad came out a few minutes later, in a silk dressing gown. She looked quizzically at me, and then asked Marie whom she had brought with her this morning to be her helper.

"I wish he were my helper," Marie said. "This is Karim, my nephew, and I brought him with me to see if you can help find him work around the campus so that he can make enough money to help himself continue his education."

Mrs. Haddad sat down and smiled at the two young people, then said she would be happy to do what she could as she was impressed with Marie's very good work and was certain her nephew would work just as hard. She then turned to me and asked me a few questions about my family and my father's work. When I explained that my father was a stonemason, Mrs. Haddad questioned why I did not choose to work with him. I replied that there was not much work at this time, and in any case, I preferred to study to be an engineer or a doctor. Mrs. Haddad said it would be terribly expensive and wondered where I could get enough funds to pay my way. I leaned forward in my seat and assured Mrs. Haddad that I was prepared to work as hard as necessary to earn enough money to pay for an education, as it was the most important thing in the world to me at this time. Mrs. Haddad could sense my determination and sincerity and promised to talk to her husband to see if he had any ideas for me. She then turned back to Marie to finish discussing the sewing that was to be done and when that business was wrapped up she went back into the house to speak to her husband, who was having breakfast in the dining room. Marie and I looked anxiously at each other but waited patiently until Mrs. Haddad returned to the verandah. She came out with a smile on her face and told me that her husband would like to see me in his office on campus at 10:30 that morning. Marie and I thanked Mrs. Haddad profusely for her assistance. I then left the two women alone to finish the sewing and walked to the school building where I planned to wait for the appointed time to meet Mr. Haddad.

The International College, the AUB affiliate high school, was for boys only and it was divided into two sections, English and French. I sat on a bench inside the main entrance and watched the students as they arrived at school, hoping all the while that I would soon be one of them. At ten o'clock, I made my way to Mr.

Haddad's office, where the secretary asked me to sit down and wait another half hour. Finally, at 10:30, the secretary invited a nervous me to follow her into Mr. Haddad's office, where I found a jovial, easygoing man who greeted me with a ready smile. Mr. Haddad was of medium height, solidly built, with short, dark hair. He welcomed me and asked me to sit down, then began asking questions about the school I had attended and the classes and the languages I had studied. I replied that I had obtained the government elementary school certificate in Arabic and French, but I had not studied any English. We talked about my language options for my high school studies, with Mr. Haddad suggesting I enter the English section, as though the decision had already been made for me to register at the high school. I could hardly believe my ears and readily agreed with Mr. Haddad. As I had no knowledge of English, Mr. Haddad advised me I would have to have an intensive English course at inter-session before I could be admitted into the high school. Again, hardly believing my luck, I heartily agreed that this would be best.

I asked Mr. Haddad about possible jobs and, after some reflection, Mr. Haddad looked sternly at me and said if I promised to work extremely hard, there would be a job waiting for me in the school kitchen and cafeteria. I jumped to my feet, unable to contain my joy, and thanked Mr. Haddad profusely and warmly for his assistance. I anxiously assured Mr. Haddad that I would be the hardest working student in either the school or the kitchen, whereupon Mr. Haddad sent me off to meet Mr. Habib, the kitchen supervisor. After a brief interview with Mr. Habib, I was assured of the job. I then ran all the way to the Haddad residence and excitedly told them of what had transpired and thanked Mrs. Haddad and my aunt Marie for their help. I then continued on to my grandmother's house to share the good news. After having lemonade and a snack to celebrate, I hugged my Grandma and thanked her for her love and assistance. I then packed up my belongings and said farewell to my grandmother, promising to return on June 15 to start inter-session.

I returned to Shweir on the bus. Amin, the driver, could see that my spirits were high and asked me what was behind my smile. I was only too happy to tell Amin about Mr. Haddad and school and my new job. Amin was happy for me, but then started to tease me about turning into an educated snob who would forget his family, friends and village roots, someone who would become absorbed in his studies and would no longer be able to converse with ordinary people, someone who would become so eccentric that his old friends would begin to consider him crazy! I took Amin's teasing seriously and started to defend myself, swearing that I would never become aloof or eccentric and would always remember my family, my friends and my roots. As the bus happened to be stopped at this point, Amin reached over and hugged me around the shoulders, and assured me that he was only teasing and knew that he and I would always be friends, no matter what.

When I finally arrived back in Shweir, I ran home to tell my parents about Mr. Haddad and the help he had given me. My parents were pleased for me even though they were worried that they would not be able to give me enough additional assistance. My sisters jumped around the house in joy when they heard my news and clamoured that they too wanted to go to school in Beirut. The next several days were spent cleaning, patching and ironing my clothes so they could be packed for school. I made a tour of Shweir to tell my friends that I would be leaving for summer school in Beirut. Some were glad for me but others said they would miss our games and escapades and they hoped I would drop out and soon return to our village and our lives of idleness and joy.

Early Monday morning, I boarded the bus for Beirut with a bag of clothes and a bag of home-made bread. When I arrived at my grandmother's house after the long trip to Beirut, I left my bags in the main room and caught the tramway to the university campus where I reported to work at the cafeteria for the International College. The head cook Habib, told me in no uncertain terms that he expected complete dedication to the cafeteria, that I was Habib's employee first and foremost, that I would have to work hard, be on time, complete all my assigned tasks and never leave until all the work was done. Habib was short, bold and husky and he looked tough and authoritarian. I answered with a brisk, "YES SIR," and got to work right away.

School began one week later. Because I had not come from a recognized school, three of my new teachers had to examine me to determine my level of learning and my abilities. They concluded that I needed two classes in fast track English, as I would need English to follow the physics and math classes, which were taught in English. I found the first two weeks extremely difficult, but after that, English began to come to me fairly quickly because of my solid grounding in French. One day, while reading a passage out loud in an English class, I came to the word "bridge" and I pronounced the middle "I" the same as one would normally pronounce "I", the personal pronoun. Every body in the class started to laugh, including the teacher who corrected me. I felt embarrassed but the teacher helped by reminding the class that there were many exceptions to the general rules of English and they would all be breaking many of them before they would become proficient.

It was while working at the cafeteria that I met Michel, another student, who was taking a math class that he had failed in the regular school year. Michel had grown up in Beirut and did not have a high opinion of students who came from rural areas. Nevertheless, Michel and I became friends and started to cooperate on our math study and assignments. Several times, I covered up for Michel at work, to give him ample time to prepare for class and exams.

Summer school lasted three months and finished with two days of final examinations. I felt I had done well but the students would not find out the results until another week had passed. In the meantime, I continued to work at the cafeteria. Some American dishes were being served and this was my first introduction to American food. Some desserts I particularly liked were apple pie á la mode and ice cream sundaes with pineapple topping.

When the marks were finally posted, I was elated to find I had done well in all of my courses. I made an appointment to see Mr. Haddad so that I could thank him for all his help and let him know that I was doing well. Mr. Haddad congratulated me on my good work and told me I would be promoted to grade 11 and expected me to continue to do as well during the next school year. I was pleased and expressed my sincere gratitude to Mr. Haddad and promised I would continue to work very hard to justify the confidence Mr. Haddad had shown in me.

I was able to go home to Shweir for the last two weeks of summer. My parents were happy to see me back at home and were pleased to learn I was doing well at school. Yet, they suggested I find a better paying job for one year, save money and then return to school after that but I told them I was determined to resume school in the upcoming fall term. My parents were not completely happy with my decision but finally told me I could do what I thought was best for me. However, my father was not making enough money to support the family so they could not help me financially. I would have to earn on my own whatever I needed to go to school. This news was crushing for me for there was no work in Shweir and what could I earn in two weeks anyway. I felt the heavens crashing down around me and thought I was about to lose sight of my dream. Several days of gloom and doom had passed when I ran into one of my summer school teachers on the main street of the summer district of Shweir. Mounir Saadeh, originally from Damascus, Syria, was a pleasant man and he stopped to chat a while with me and to ask me if I was planning to register for the fall term. I hesitated before answering Mr. Saadeh's question, and then finally decided to tell him the truth and explain that I might not be able to afford to return to school. Mr. Saadeh continued to ask questions until he learned from me that my parents could not assist me financially. After a short silence that seemed like hours to me Mr. Saadeh asked me to come see him tomorrow at his summer hostel at Ain El Kassis, one of the more secluded areas of the village. I felt hopeful that the coincidental meeting could lead to something that would help me continue my education, but my heart still felt heavy and I was afraid to expect too much from the next day's appointment.

The next day, I went to the hostel at 10:00 to meet Mr. Saadeh. After a few pleasantries, Mr. Saadeh asked me how much money I needed to return to school. I estimated I would need LL200.00. Mr. Saadeh nodded, and then told me he could lend me LL100.00 and if I could find the rest from somewhere else, I would be able to return to school. I thanked Mr. Saadeh profusely saying I was determined to get all the money I needed and I would talk to my parents again about ways to get the balance. I left a few minutes later, feeling very happy that Mr. Saadeh was willing to help me. I hurried home to tell my mother about Mr. Saadeh's offer and begged her to convince my father to help me somehow. My mother cried and promised to talk to my father after supper to see what they could do.

My father came home late from work, but I waited patiently until he had finished his supper before telling him about Mr. Saadeh's offer and asking for help. My father remained silent, serene and absorbed in his thoughts. My mother finally broke the silence and said they had to find some way to help me return to school. My father finally spoke, saying that his work was not going well this summer and he did not know if they would have enough money to buy provisions for the winter, let alone help me go to school. The three of us then talked for a long time about the grim economic conditions caused by the war until my mother suggested we could sell her wedding necklace and use part of the money to help me. She said it would be an opportune time "to spend the white money saved for the black day!" After a few more minutes of discussion, my father agreed to sell the jewellery. All three of us felt better at having arrived at a solution to the problem and I told my parents how grateful I was for their sacrifice and their love and I promised to do very well in school. I also vowed I would never again have to ask my parents for financial assistance.

A few days later, my father and I took my mother's necklace to the jewellery market in Beirut where we were able to sell it for LL265.00. It was a lovely 24-karat gold necklace set with several rubies. Both my father and I cried after we left the jeweller's store. But we went together to the International College where we met Mr. Saadeh and told him we had been able to find the money to help me return to school. Mr. Saadeh was pleased to hear the news and told my father that the money for my education would be the best investment for the future that he could possibly make. I then went to register for the fall semester and to buy the necessary books before returning with my father to Sitto Nabiha's house. We were warmly greeted by Nabiha and her children and after sharing some coffee and sweets my father said good-bye to everyone and returned to Shweir, leaving me at my grandmother's.

Once school started, I commuted daily on the tramway from the east side of Beirut to the west side where the International

College was located. The tramway ride took 40 minutes and I had to walk about 20 minutes from Nabiha's house to the nearest station, so each day I spent two hours getting to and from school. As I had to start work at 7:30 in the morning at the cafeteria, I left the house each morning at 6:00 to make sure I got to work on time. Once at the cafeteria, my job was to collect the dirty dishes and wash them and occasionally to serve food if one of the cooks was ill or on vacation. During the lunch hour, the routine was basically the same, although sometimes I would be asked to help serve tables in the faculty dining room, which was adjacent to the student cafeteria. One of the benefits of working in the cafeteria was that I could eat for free whatever was not sold. I ended up with the same meal more often than not — white bean stew and rice. It was nutritious and filling but always gave me a bad case of gas. My aunts and uncle, who shared the same room with me at Nabiha's house, promised me a treat and begged me to skip my lunch at the cafeteria to spare them the aftereffects, but I really had little choice.

The school year passed quickly and smoothly for me, and I did well in all my courses. I was particularly interested in the political discussions about the situation in the Middle East and would mull over the history teacher's ideas that the best thing for the region would be to invite all the kings, the princes, the presidents and the prime ministers together for a sumptuous dinner party on a ship and once everybody had eaten their fill and had drunk to their hearts' satisfaction to sink the ship.

I was also influenced by the books I was reading in class, including a biography of Abraham Lincoln that described his poverty, hard work, his drive to abolish slavery and his belief in government of the people, by the people and for the people. His beliefs and his assassination were ingrained into my mind and helped form my views of the role of individuals in their society and the world. I also read the books of Gibran Khalil Gibran, who wrote about love, morality, religion, politics and life in the Middle East and his immigration to the United States influenced my outlook about myself and life in general.

After completing my academic year, I was able to find a job for the summer. I started working in West Hall on the AUB campus as a clerk-receptionist for the American soldiers who were attending orientation courses before being posted to Middle Eastern spots. It was the best paying job I had ever had so I was able to save enough for the next school year and also help my parents buy provisions for the winter. It turned out that my contributions accounted for at least half of what the family was able to buy. Although I would have liked to go home for a visit, I stayed in Beirut to be able to save the greatest possible amount of money.

The American soldiers had a social coordinator, Mrs. Stone, who arranged dances, religious services, field trips to the Cedars of Lebanon, historical cities and sites, and even dinner invitations for the soldiers. She was efficient and well-known in the community. She often asked me to volunteer my time and help her organize some of the events, and I was happy to oblige. One day, Mrs. Stone asked me to pick up and deliver some paper ornaments to her house that she planned to use to decorate for a party. It was a warm Saturday afternoon and when I arrived I found Mrs. Stone dressed informally in shorts and sleeveless shirt. She invited me to come in and asked for my help in putting up the decorations. I tried to come up with excuses to avoid coming in the house, but Mrs. Stone was determined that I should help her and eventually I reluctantly agreed to come in. Mrs. Stone brought out a stepladder and explained to me that she would stand on the ladder and I was to hold the ladder and hand her the decorations and thumb tacks she would use to pin the decorations on the wall. It took the two of us about half an hour to complete the job and when it was over Mrs. Stone climbed down from the step ladder, threw herself on me, grabbed me and started to kiss me. I blushed and felt perplexed by her behaviour but I was determined to leave so I gently extricated myself from Mrs. Stone's arms and backed out her door. Once I was outside, I ran all the way to the tramway station and returned to my grandmother's house. I spent the rest of the day wondering whether I had done the right thing, but by recalling the teachings of the priest and the novels of Khalil Gibran, I was finally able to comfort myself that my behaviour had been proper in the circumstances. The next day, when I saw Mrs. Stone at work, I looked away and tried to avoid her, but at the first opportunity when we were alone in the office, Mrs. Stone came over to me and apologized for what she had done. I did not know what to say and although I tried to forget the whole thing, I found I was more comfortable avoiding Mrs. Stone as much as I could for the remainder of the summer.

One additional incident that summer stuck out in my mind. In my spare time I was tutoring mathematics to two high school girls. One of the young girls developed a crush on me. I knew I could not get side-tracked from my education and the need to make enough money to go back to school, so I decided to remove myself from the situation and told the girl's mother I could not teach her any more due to a scheduling conflict.

When summer was over, I returned to International College to complete my grade 12. I was beginning to feel confident that I would be able to enter university the next year. I followed the same routine I had in grade 11, working in the cafeteria, taking courses and riding the tramway and eschewing all entertainment. One of my grade 12 teachers, Mr. Waring, was an American and a member of the American armed forces stationed in Lebanon that year. His responsibility was to coordinate social events for the armed forces but through his friendship with Mr. Leavitt, the director of the school, he was asked to teach an English literature class. One day, he was explaining one of the passages in a novel, which included the words "Gone with the Wind"; he asked who could explain the passage? I understood the actual meaning of the words but could not explain their significance in the passage. Mr. Waring was pleased when I volunteered an answer to his question, then he asked the class who had seen the movie, "Gone with the Wind". Every student put up their hand except me; I had not had an evening out during my entire time in Beirut.

Late in the year, Mr. Waring asked me to stay after class one day to speak to me. After all the other students had left, Mr. Waring asked me if I were planning to attend the graduation ceremonies. When I said I would not be able to, Mr. Waring said he thought I should attend and if I was not planning to go only because I did not have a suit, then he was going to give me a suit he had just bought because he was being transferred to England and the suit would not be appropriate for the English weather. I was taken aback and did not want to accept the offer, but Mr. Waring insisted and assured me that I would be denying him a pleasure if his offer were refused. As I stood there, I realized that I had worn the same two pairs of khaki pants, patched and faded, during the entire school year and finally agreed to accept the gift, thanking Mr. Waring profusely. I said I would be proud to attend graduation wearing a suit from one of my teachers, but, unfortunately, as it turned out, Mr. Waring had to leave Beirut before the graduation ceremony was held and did not see me walk proudly across the stage.

During that winter, a nationalist movement began spreading the idea that scientific and commonly accepted foreign words should be translated from English and French into Arabic so that everyone could understand and use them in order to protect the integrity of the Arabic language. Most of the Middle Eastern states were agitating for independence and one of the main goals was to have the freedom to speak and write in Arabic in all circumstances. An ad-hoc committee was struck by the nationalist group to translate into Arabic all foreign words that had infiltrated the daily language, words such as ice cream, sandwich, cinema, automobile, and pass, which was used by tramway riders to indicate they had paid for one month unlimited travel on the tramway. I found the exercise a little silly, particularly when I learned that sandwich was to be translated as "al shatter wal mashtoor wabinahooma al kamekh". I decided to write a short article for the student newspaper making fun of the committee's efforts and I titled my article "Pass". The article described an incident that had supposedly taken place on the tramway and described how Abu Khalil, a farmer, had come into Beirut to visit his son, who was a student at AUB. The tramway he took to AUB was full of students and the conductor was checking who needed travel tickets. All the students answered his requests for the fare in Arabic, saying "Mitjawez", which meant, "I am carrying a pass". When the farmer, who had been observing the responses of the students, was asked for the fare, he responded, "Ana kaman mitjawez," which literally meant, "I'm married too." In my article, the conductor laughed and shouted to the students on the tramway and said, "Abu Khalil is also mitjawez (married)," and the joke spread throughout the tramway, until everyone was shouting out loud together, "Abu Khalil Metjawez!"

When the school year was finally over, the graduation ceremony was held in the open air, on the hockey field, and my grandmother, Nabiha, and my uncle Sabih and my Aunts Marie and Badre attended. I was happy to have completed my grade 12 and thanked Mr. Haddad, Mr. Saadeh, my grandmother, my aunts and my uncle for their tremendous help, which made it possible for me to graduate from the International College. I thanked them all for encouraging me to carry on to the American University of Beirut to earn a degree in my chosen field of engineering which I completed in five years.

After graduation, I worked for the Trans Arabian Pipe Line Company for two years in construction but I always felt deep within me that it was greener on the western side of the Atlantic Ocean, since my grandfather, his sisters Nabiha and Haifa, several of his relatives: the Naders, the Shayas, the Toumas, the Khenaissers, the Sawayas and their families, all lived in the USA. I applied for and was awarded a scholarship to the University of Kansas, so I decided to go to the United States. I boarded a plane as the sun was rising and colouring up the sky. Once the plane took off I glanced back at the Beirut skyline and the sea. As the sun's rays began to glint off the windows, the city appeared to be bathed in gold. It nearly broke my heart to see how beautiful Beirut looked from the plane. However, as the plane flew off, I remembered the song I used to sing as a child, about the bird who preferred the danger and beauty of an unfettered life in the forest to the secure and jailed life of the gilded cage. The childhood memory made me smile and, as Beirut became smaller and smaller in the distance, I knew I had made the right decision and was on my way to achieve my dream. I did not foresee then, that my future included becoming a professor, engineer, researcher, inventor, developer, and entrepreneur and philanthropist.

Photographs

29. Nahr Abu Dawood river, 1994
30. Abu Dawood's grandson Anwar and me on the way to Miami, Arizona, Photo by A. G. Kenicer, 2004
31. International College, 1994
32. Kitchen in International College, 1994
33. American University of Beirut, Photo by John Waterbury, AUB president 2004
34. My son John and me, West Hall, AUB Campus, 1994
35. New residential area in Ramleh Baida white sand district, Beirut, Photo by Telko Sport, 1984
36. The famous rock Rawsheh Pigeon Grotto, Beirut, Photo by Telko Sport, 1984
37. My Departure to the USA, 1951
38. The K-Slump and Flow Tester, 1973
39. The K-Slump used in the CN Tower, Toronto, *Saskatoon StarPhoenix*, 1974
40. Flipping Wheatkey Burger, *Saskatoon StarPhoenix*, 1974
41. A danger of chauvinism, Editor, *Saskatoon StarPhoenix*, 1973
42. Man with a Vision. Murray Lyons, *Saskatoon StarPhoenix*, 1999
43. The Good Neighbour, Beverly Fast, *Green & White, University of Saskatchewan Alumni Magazine*, 2005
44. F1 - Karim, 1932
45. F2 - My Departure to the USA, 1951
46. B1 - May M. Nasser
47. B2 - Karim (Kay) W. Nasser

Index